Around the world in vintage
holiday brochures

Holiday Exotica

JONNY TRUNK

FUEL

GOING ANYWHERE NICE?

JONNY TRUNK

Back in the 1970s, holidays meant very little for my family. We never went abroad, never stayed in hotels – it was my mother's firm and unswervable opinion that 'abroad' was full of foreign people she did not understand, and foreign food she did not want to taste. She was happy at home in Britain, among the British, making spaghetti bolognese, lasagne or moussaka. Consequently, our annual summer holiday would be one of two experiences:

i) my two sisters and I would be put on a train to Norfolk at Liverpool Street station, left in the care of a kind-looking stranger. We would be met at Norwich station by our grannie and spend the following five weeks at her failing farm in Norfolk. Our days were packed with activities: falling into ditches, exploring broken farm machinery, being stung by nettles, watching pigs, watching rats, getting our clothing caught on barbed wire and (if we'd behaved ourselves) a possible visit to the fun fair at Great Yarmouth.

ii) spending a week with our parents in a rented holiday cottage my mother had found in the back pages of *The Lady* magazine. These cottages were always in one of three locations – Devon, Cumbria or Yorkshire. (If the Yorkshire option, then it would have to be in the area where the television series *All Creatures Great and Small* (1978–1980) was shot.) For a young boy these holiday cottages meant incarceration in a rural, remote and unfamiliar location, often with crap English weather, with the budget for a small Airfix model that would be completed on day one. I recall one holiday where, after a seven-hour, pre-motorway, carsick-inducing drive (all five of us plus luggage in a Mini Clubman estate), we arrived at our destination cottage, in the village of Lowther, near Penrith. My mother got out of the car and, rather than let out a sigh of relief that we'd finally arrived after a difficult journey, she got straight back in, demanding we return home immediately, as there was a funny farmyard smell in the area. This was most likely because the cottage she had rented was next door to a farm.

Once we had settled in, mandatory daily excursions would start. These always included a trip to local museums and any – or all – National Trust homes within a 30-minute drive. Looking back on these holidays I'm filled with a nostalgic gloom. Fortunately, no such gloom is featured anywhere in this book. This is a collection of happy holiday brochures, travel guides, maps, railway timetables, airline publications, hotel info and more – promising escape, joy, sunshine, even a taste of paradise.

I stumbled across a 1960s map of the Lake District (opposite) with an abstract, graphic simplicity that appealed to me. So I started looking into maps and printed travel ephemera. After discovering more examples at an antiques market, my vintage-wired brain automatically took me to 1960s and 1970s holiday brochures – the type that were never considered, or even allowed, in our house when I was growing up. These would have lined the shelves of the local Thomas Cook or Thomson's travel agencies on the high street. Sun-drenched getaways were always advertised on TV immediately after Christmas, with warm promises of lovely times, crystal-clear seas and more lovely times. Looking back, the only other occasion you might chance upon such exotic holidays was when they appeared on gameshows. The 'Holiday of a Lifetime' (plus spending money) to a desert island paradise or (less often) a hotbed of cultural history were the always unreachable jackpot prizes in shows like *Sale of the Century* (1971–1983), *3-2-1* (1978–1988) and *The Price Is Right* (1984–1988). And of course ITV also had the weekly seasonal travel show *Wish You Were Here...?* (1974–2003), an opportunity for my mother to sit in front of the TV and slag off the presenter Judith Chalmers' floaty summer dresses, or the hotels and beaches she would be showing off. Such holidays were out of reach for many. But not everything in this book is about luxury and money. The travel industry catered for all places and all pockets. As a result, collecting material for the book took me in local, as well as global, directions, across land, sea and air.

BARTHOLOMEW
LAKE
DISTRICT
One inch
map
cloth 50p

I quickly realised that holiday brochures, particularly early post-war ones, were pretty scarce. For obvious reasons there were few holiday companies during this period, so few were produced. When I did find some from the late 1950s and 1960s, they had little visual merit. So I was forced to broaden my hunt for material. I started digging up information on coach trips, railway pamphlets, camping leaflets, travel maps, hotel brochures, timetables for all sorts of transport, youth hostel guides and more. As the collection expanded I began thinking about how we arrived in this particular departure lounge. Back in the middle of last century, travel was not for the faint hearted. If you had enough money then luxury cruises, classy airplanes and exclusive hotels with fine services and expertise awaited you.

At the other end of the spectrum, there were the joys of camping or caravanning, both in the UK and Europe. With help from the youth hostel network and organised international sites, you had the option of travelling in your own car, via fly drive or channel ferry links. Or you could take a coach, sharing a British or international trip with around 40 other people in a large noisy vehicle with no air conditioning and, until relatively recently, no toilet. My first ever holiday abroad was in 1983, to Lloret de Mar on the Costa Brava, Spain. It started (and ended) with a shocking 36-hour coach journey that quickly descended into whiffy chaos when the on-board loo malfunctioned early after only 100 miles. It was fascinating to find that some of the coach companies featured in this book are still active (like Vista), proving that the coach holiday is still very much a pillar of the British tourist industry.

I also had a strong desire to find boating holiday brochures for places like the Norfolk Broads (no doubt due to our holidays with our grannie in Norfolk). The 'boating holiday' was one of my many childhood holiday fantasies, mainly because at that time, some of the larger cruisers looked so great, with long fibreglass or wooden curves and sliding cabin roofs. The thought of sleeping on water, anchored in some remote, silent corner of a waterway, seemed idyllic. The closest my family ever got was a day trip in Wroxham, where my dad managed to broadside a much bigger vessel directly underneath a narrow bridge. Everyone looked down at us from the top of the bridge and laughed. My dad couldn't restart our little boat's engine so we just floated along, going nowhere – but very much in the way of everyone, until we were finally rescued by the hire company. Unfortunately it turned out that boating and waterway brochures were as illusive as my father's seamanship.

However, those for cruises were easier to locate and I found that they made for interesting reading. At the time, these were sold as unusual and sophisticated, high-end holidays (some costing a whopping £343), but the photographs show small yachts, passenger ships for a limited number of passengers. They appear positively quaint in comparison to their contemporaries – those obscene monsters of the sea, packed with thousands of hungry and demanding travellers, who spend two weeks afloat, sampling a selection of pools, slides, casinos, all you can eat restaurants, soft-play zones, bars, discos, cinemas, gyms, shops and every other possible convenience to keep them and their kids occupied at sea, but sort of on a floating land for two weeks. As the propellers slowly churn the ocean waves full of their 'black water.'

We can also see the slow development of the package holiday, from both here in the UK and abroad. Companies like Butlin's, with its all-inclusive experience, were already long established and clearly had a clientele that would come back year after year. I uncovered several great souvenir postcards, which were way more interesting than their fairly pedestrian and repetitive brochures. Some classic 'wish you were here' comments, had been scrawled on the reverse, and I've included these in the captions for your amusement.

It was also fascinating to see developments in how different countries approached their marketing. While Sweden was busy promoting cruises and skiing, Australia seemed to have a unique aptitude for producing remarkably cool, graphic-themed literature for parks and cities. As for the USA and Canada, these countries were built for tourism. Hunting, shooting and fishing were well catered for, as were the large number of wild parks and breathtaking landscapes. I found leaflets for craters, waterfalls, dams, bear parks, even an underwater fairyland. Alongside these are various leaflets for classic New York attractions, including the World Trade Center and its unforgettable viewing deck, reminding me once more of valuable memories and vistas.

Considering the entire spectrum of material I found, that produced by airlines provided some of the most vivid graphics – timetables, directions and route maps – the presentation of such potentially dull information was actually the perfect opportunity for designers to utilise an imaginative range of eye-popping modern ideas. Throughout the book it is apparent that budget constraints were no constraint for the imagination; limited colours combined with strong logos can produce stunning designs, concepts and formats.

I found it hard to ignore the Anglo-French triumph that was Concorde, such was its revolutionary appearance and time-saving sexiness. After discovering a couple of impressive brochures demonstrating the sleek elegance of the aircraft, I had to put the brakes on – before I lost myself down the runway of overpriced Concorde collectables.

As you peruse these pages, please remember that the brochures are from a time when there were no smartphones, no internet, no easy international communications, no instant digital maps to follow, no QR Code tickets on your phone, no credit cards either! Good tourism was the result of serious organisation: local currency, maps, fold-out guides, timetables you had to read and try to understand, it required dedication.

Full research was often necessary and was supplied through the extensive brochures and related literature presented in this publication. The tourists who used these brochures hungered for authentic experiences from the countries they visited. They craved detailed information to gain a fuller understanding of a place, not just a vacuous phone snap for their social media.

How times have changed. On my last holiday to Majorca, we arrived around 8.30am at a small beach in a conservation area (because I love swimming in the sea in the mornings on holiday, it's one of my 'things'). Even at that early hour, there was a queue to climb down through the rocks, which were infested with content creators and social media personalities, busy making short films, before heading off to the next location for their next silly performance. It was one of the oddest and saddest things I've ever seen.

Of course it is an impossible task to circumnavigate the entire world globe through holiday brochures, but the examples presented here do cover a large chunk. They most date from between 1955 and 1985, a period roughly bookended by post-war affluence and the arrival of the internet. Today our lives are online, along with our bookings, digital tickets and emailed itinerary information: in the future the glorious travel ephemera captured in these pages will simply not exist. But I'm betting that coaches will still be running all around the world – and you can almost guarantee that the loo will malfunction.

See you on holiday!

Page 5: Lake District Map, 1971
A one-inch-scale cloth map made by John Bartholomew of Edinburgh. Complete with an interesting and informative essay about ancient settlers.

Page 6: Holidays Abroad, 1963
A 'Take Home Book'. Having read this informative guide I can tell you that Mr Cash's travel advice is still relevant seven decades later. I'm a big fan of these effective white dots.

Page 7: Odd Spot, 1965
25 articles about Yorkshire hamlets, including Thwing, Crackpot, Paull and Booze. Yes, there's a hamlet called Booze. What a superbly simple and unexpected graphic treatment.

Left: Span, 1965
A short-lived package dealer soon gobbled up by more aggressive UK travel companies in a rapidly expanding sector of the industry.

Above: BOAC, 1969
Printed guides for various British Overseas Airways Corporation (BOAC) destinations were available free on board their aircraft. These included polar and Siberia routes. Such clean, paired-back travel graphics are difficult to beat.

Page 10: Gatwick Airport London, 1976
The name Gatwick derives from old English for goat (*gat*) and farm, (*wik*). So it's a goat farm. The groovy hand-drawn font certainly makes me feel welcome.

WELCOME
Gatwick Airport London

CONTENTS

Air Alsace, 1974
A distinctive brochure from a small airline based in Strasbourg. After several mergers they ceased trading in 1981.

Air Dauphine, c.1964
This has to be one of the oddest leaflets in this collection as it seems to have no purpose, it only features what you can see here. Perhaps this is the reason behind the airline's failure after a mere six years.

Aeroflot TU-154, 1970
A brochure promoting the new Russian-built Tupolev jet, which remained in production until 2013.

Overleaf: Various international timetables dating from 1961–1984. Some truly great design elements here. Superb fonts, lively use of arrows and curves – striking graphic forms that really imply dynamic movement.

April 29, 1979
System Flight Directory
Southern

HAWAIIAN AIR
TIMETABLE
EFFECTIVE: OCTOBER 25, 1981
NO. 210
SUPER80

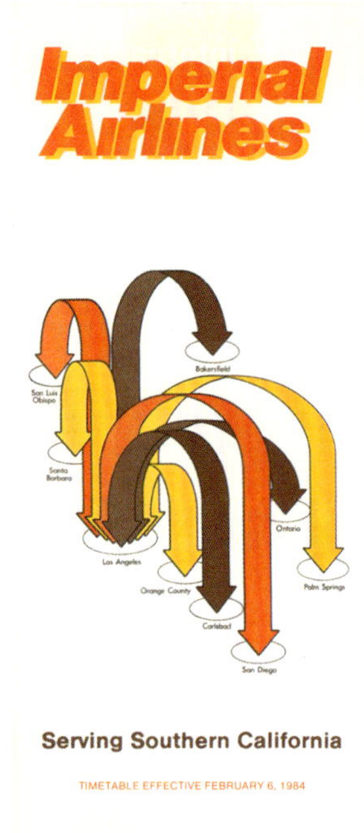
Imperial Airlines
Bakersfield
San Luis Obispo
Santa Barbara
Ontario
Los Angeles
Palm Springs
Orange County
Carlsbad
San Diego
Serving Southern California
TIMETABLE EFFECTIVE FEBRUARY 6, 1984

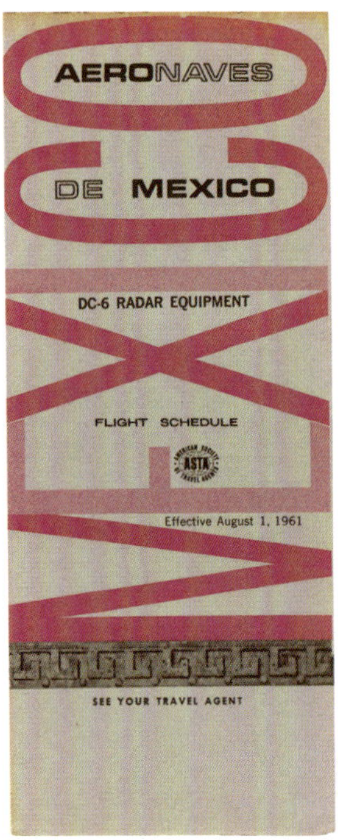
AERONAVES
DE MEXICO
MEXICO
DC-6 RADAR EQUIPMENT
FLIGHT SCHEDULE
ASTA
Effective August 1, 1961
SEE YOUR TRAVEL AGENT

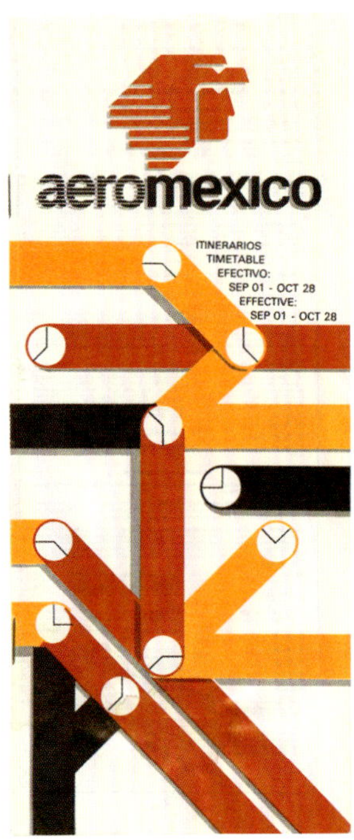
aeromexico
ITINERARIOS
TIMETABLE
EFECTIVO:
SEP 01 - OCT 28
EFFECTIVE:
SEP 01 - OCT 28

PSA
PACIFIC SOUTHWEST AIRLINES
Flight Schedule
EFFECTIVE
OCTOBER 1, 1973
SACRAMENTO
SAN FRANCISCO
OAKLAND
SAN JOSE
STOCKTON
FRESNO
HOLLYWOOD-BURBANK
LOS ANGELES
ONTARIO
LONG BEACH
SAN DIEGO
Schedule subject to change without notice

SKYWAYS international
SUMMER TIMETABLE
1971
HORAIRES D'ETE
LONDON VIA ASHFORD TO
PARIS CLERMONT-FERRAND
MONTPELLIER & OSTEND
LUTON TO OSTEND
EAST MIDLANDS TO PARIS
MARCH 26th to OCTOBER 31st
26 MARS au 31 OCTOBRE

CANADA
vacation weather
AIR CANADA
ADV-2053

SWISSAIR
Worldwide
Timetable
Winter 1975
Second Edition
Effective January 1, 1975
Next edition: April 1, 1975

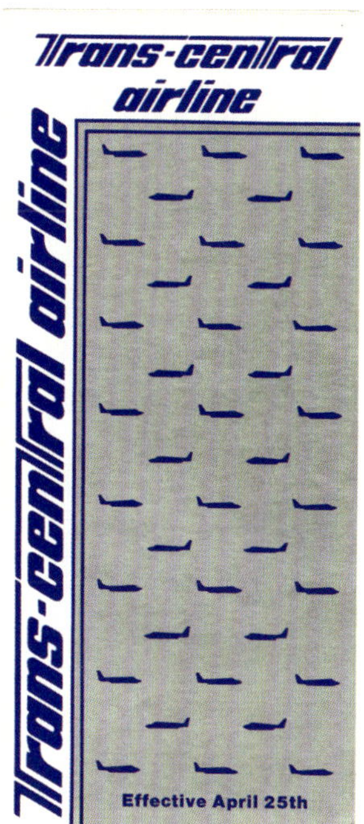
Trans-central
airline
Trans-central airline
Effective April 25th

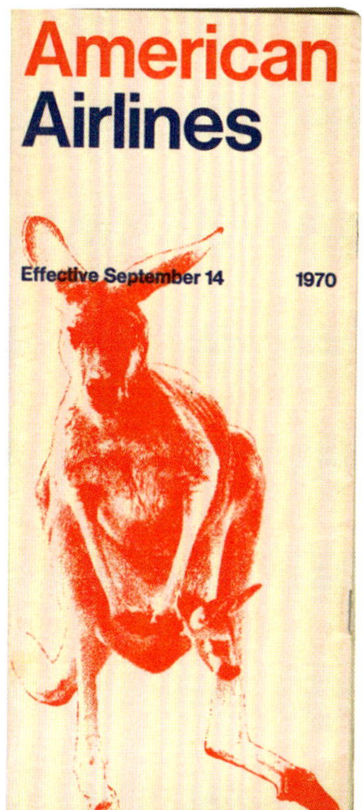
American
Airlines
Effective September 14
1970

AmericanAirlines
Directions

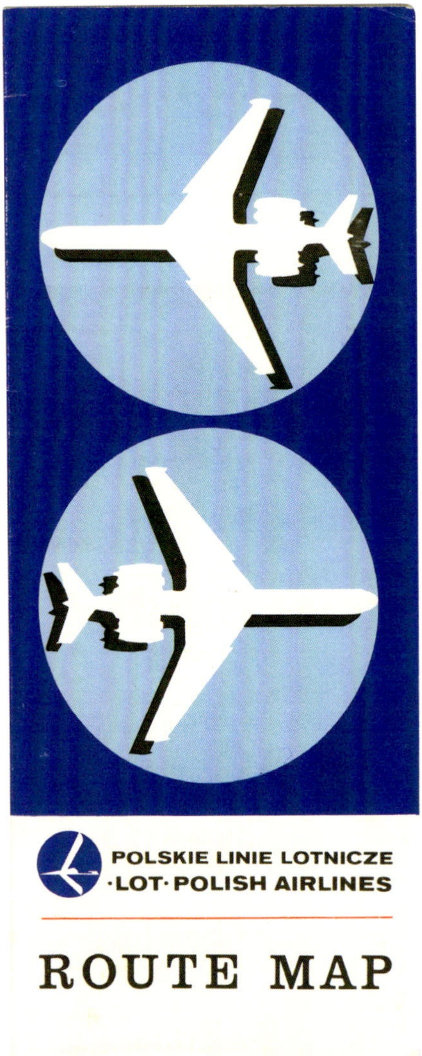

Polish Airlines Route Map, c.1968
A fine map and directory from the late 1960s, printed by the Polish State Cartographic Services.

Olympic Route Maps, late 1960s
A compact and economic set of maps for Athens-based airline.

Concorde Air France, 1975
This influential brochure for Air France uses the aircraft logo and wordmark created by French typographer Roger Excoffon (1910–1983) and is designed by the SYNELOG studio.

Air France Concorde, 1978
A pocket guide to international destinations covered by Concorde.

Concorde British Airways, 1970s
'Arrive before you leave. Flying at over twice the speed of sound.' Containing in-flight information and history of the supersonic superstar. Due to the speed (faster than the Earth's rotation) and time difference, passengers flying west from London to New York experienced the phenomenon of arriving at a similar time to their departure.

CONCORDE
British airways

CAL-STATE
AIR LINES
"WE'VE GOT CONNECTIONS"
FLIGHT
SCHEDULE
EFFECTIVE
JULY 18, 1969

FRONTIER
AIRLINES
EFFECTIVE JANUARY 1, 1969
Take a Summer
Vacation This Winter
Fly Frontier to Phoenix,
Las Vegas and Tucson
NOW FLYING THE ARROW-JET SUPER 727

Cal-State Airlines, 1969
Both a flight schedule and hip fashion manual by the looks of things.

Frontier Airlines, 1969
Every internal flight for every plane from January 1969 is here in a spreadsheet. I'm not sure they intended to make the leaflet look like an old paper bag with those stripes, but it works.

Braniff International, 1965
This promotional card was made to celebrate Braniff's new stewardess 'couture' outfits, designed by Emilio Pucci (1914–1992). The cabin-crew girls would make four outfit changes on every flight, from plastic departure helmet (or 'rain domes') to after-dinner culottes.

BEA About Your Flight, 1962
This in-flight information and souvenir brochure features a remarkably calm layout (undoubtedly deliberate) from the 'red square airline'.

BEA Fartplan, 1969
Always comforting to have a fartplan on a short-haul flight.

BOAC Summer Schedules, 1970
Includes polar routes and Siberia routes.

British Airways Fly-Drive, 1976
Available cars included the Volkswagen Beetle, Morris Marina and Ford Capri. A great period Magic Marker illustration in a loose style.

BOAC
SUMMER SCHEDULES
EFFECTIVE 2ND JUNE 1970
INCLUDING BOAC'S NEW SIBERIAROUTE

British airways fly-drive
1976
Fly the flag
British airways

BOAC Departures Guide, early 1970s

BOAC 747, 1970
Marking the beginning of the 'Jumbo Jet' era.

BOAC Travellers Digest, 1967
This comprehensive reference book covers numerous tourist topics including: places, people, weather, scenery, clothes, food, nightclubs, shopping, getting about, sport, museums and festivals.

TRAVELLERS
DIGEST
BOAC guide to six continents

Eastern Timetables, 1970
Two graphically exciting publications – using dynamic collage and complementary colours. Sadly nothing inside but dreary pages of dates, flight and arrival times.

Air Florida, 1979
A lovely flowing logo for this flight schedule detailing domestic 'sunshine flights' every hour, on the quarter hour.

Air France, The Express, 1967
New, comfortable, long-haul economy cabins, that 'stocky men are pleased with', or so the interior of the brochure tells us.

SAS City Portraits, Cairo, 1959
A surprisingly quirky and concise guide for the time, all the information is still pretty much relevant today.

Caledonian Airways, 1969
'Cigarettes are welcome, but pipe smoking and cigars do seem unpleasant to some, including children.' In addition, please empty your fountain pen before take off. It might explode.

Dan-Air Skyways Summer Timetable, 1973
This brochure presents simple, but rather confusing timetables. It seems most flights departed on Wednesdays.

National Airlines Route Map, 1974
Containing exhaustive maps of world-wide flights. The Sun illustrations used on the cover came courtesy of The Bettman Archive in New York.

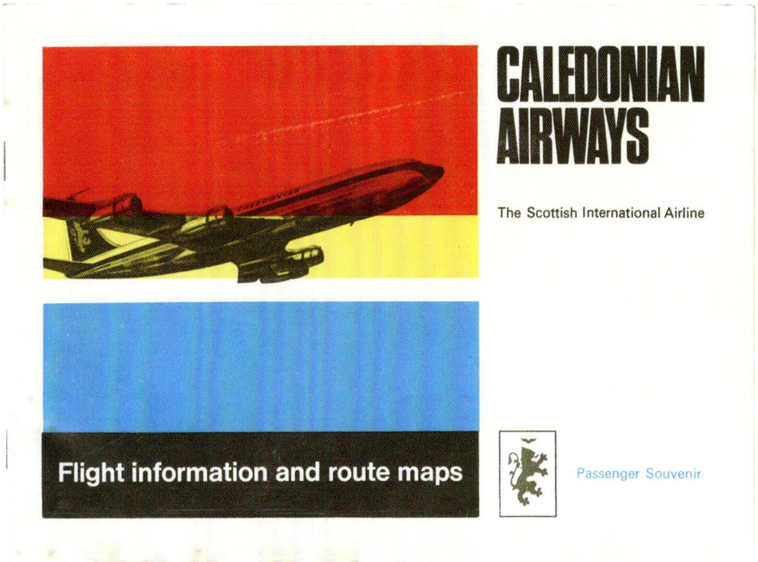
CALEDONIAN AIRWAYS
The Scottish International Airline
Flight information and route maps
Passenger Souvenir

DAN-AIR SKYWAYS
1973
ADVANCE SUMMER TIMETABLE
HOLIDAY SERVICES
1st April — 31st October

National Airlines route map
DOMESTIC/INTERNATIONAL

Quantus Pacific Routes, 1970
A 'Welcome On Board' guide complete with a pull-out cocktail menu that celebrates 50 years of the airline.

KLM Flight Companion, c.1965
An extremely useful in-flight guide in ten languages. I had no idea all KLM flights had hat racks on board.

Quantus Timetable, 1962
Amazing to think that even back then, Quantus had over 75 international offices.

Quantus Flight Guide, early 1970s
Quantus 707 jets were equipped with a library of books, magazines, chess, draughts, playing cards and airmail writing paper, for writing your mail while in the air.

QANTAS
PACIFIC ROUTES
FLIGHT GUIDE
50

QANTAS
The Australian Airline
FLIGHT GUIDE

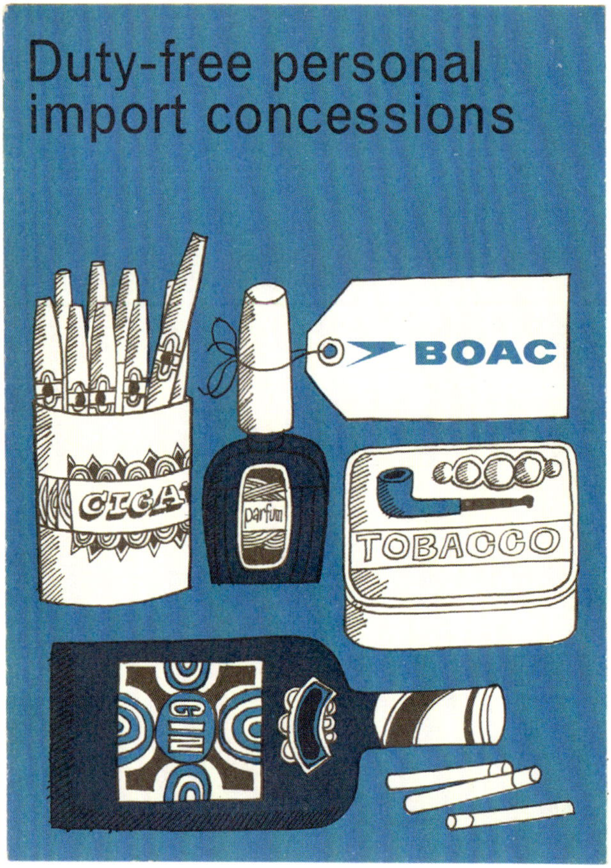

BOAC Duty Free, 1967
Wow, you could take 400 cigarettes into Australia and 400 on the way out too! These illustrations are reminiscent of the classic cookbooks by Len Deighton (1929–2026).

British European Airways, 1963
A pamphlet listing all the dos and dont's of international duty free shopping. More drawings that could be straight from a 1960s children's annual.

Duty Free Shop Düsseldorf, 1969
Those were the days, when 200 Camel, Marlboro or Rothmans cigarettes were a mere 10 Deutschmarks.

Duty Free Shop
Flughafen München

Preisliste · Pricelist 1969
DUTY
free
Shop
DÜSSELDORF

South Africa, 1970
Come and discover South Africa before everyone else does. Holidays in National Parks, ranging from 17 days to 6 weeks.

How to See the World, 1968
According to this brochure, 'The world's darkest and most mysterious continent has now become the brightest on the tourist map'.

Mombasa Beach Hotel, 1974
White sand, hot sun, skin diving. All this while you wait for another sensational lunch from the cordon bleu chef.

Nairobi, 1969
Interestingly, this brochure recommends that the shooting of wildlife should be performed using a Leica or a Pentax, rather than a gun.

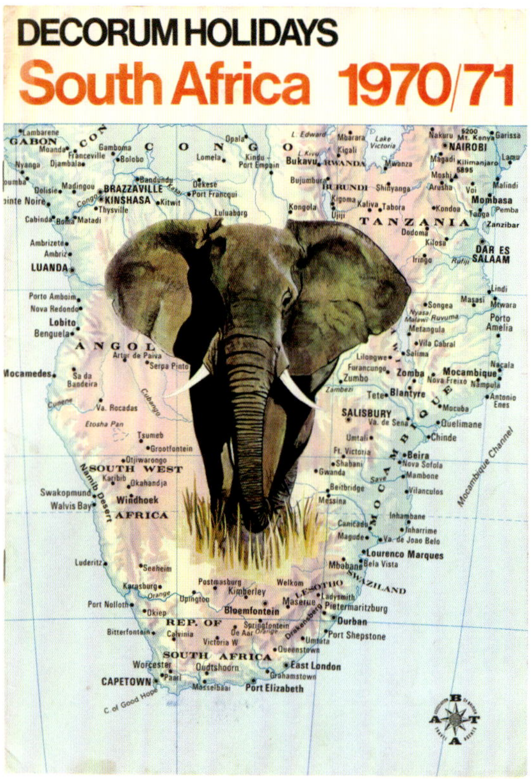

Mombasa
Beach
Hotel
now
you
can
discover
the
magic
of
tropical
Africa

NAIROBI
The Safari and Conference
Centre in Africa

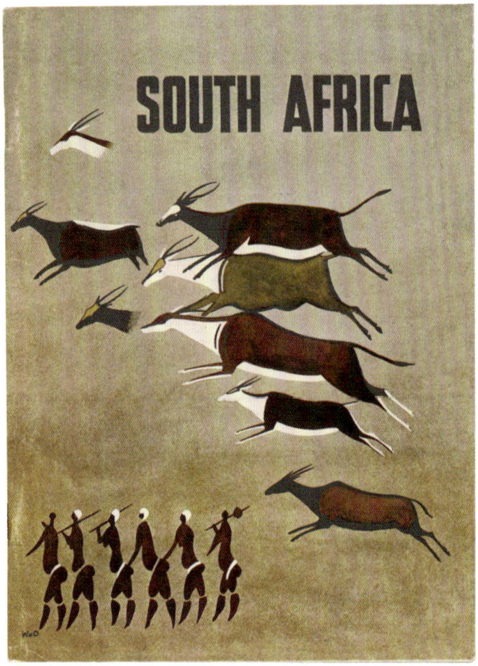

Left: South Africa, 1964
Produced by the South African State Information Bureau. The most interesting section explains the ancient drawings of 'primitive bushmen' shown on the cover.

Below: South Africa, c.1967
This early government brochure promotes the truly wild flora and fauna, with links to travel and first-class accommodation.

Springbok Safaris, 1973
'Start living life to the full. Sit Back and relax'. These slightly confusing instructions are from the brochure's opening paragraph.

Uganda Welcomes You to Sunshine!, 1972
This leaflet promoting the 'Pearl of Africa' (a term coined by Winston Churchill) has a large fold out, to show off its varied charms.

WE'D LIKE TO
DRIVE YOU WILD
on an exciting fun-filled Springbok Safaris
Luxury Coach Holiday
Springbok
Safaris

UGANDA
WELCOMES YOU TO SUNSHINE!

Around & About Fiji, 1966
This local brochure was funded by advertisers, so it contains scant tourist information, but loads about tape machines, hi-fi, beer, Parker pens and slide projectors.

Bush Camping, 1978
An international guide (in three languages) to bush camping on crown land. It's worth knowing that camping under red gum trees is potentially hazardous, as their branches fall without warning.

Adelaide, c.1950s
A fine example of incongruous collaging here, using some lovely period, hand-tinted imagery. The booklet was produced in the historic, gold-mining town of Gympie.

ADELAIDE

AUSTRALIA
Holiday Guide
You haven't seen anything yet.

Australia Holiday Guide, 1982
A large and hugely informative annual magazine, produced by the Australia Tourist Commission. The upside-down title is obvious, but still very effective.

Sydney and Suburbs, 1968
New South Wales Tourism information. $5 for a double room, complete with floorshow.

Pacific Beautizone, early 1960s
Australia's mid- north-coast holiday wonderland. 'Four seasons of sunshine' sounds good to me.

Melbourne Travellers' Guide, 1970
A fine city founded by a guy called John Batman (1801–1839). One of the few publications to have the apostrophe in the right place.

Melbourne Day Tours, 1975
A series of bus tours, including the Fairy Penguin Parade excursion to nearby Phillip Island, where the birds can be viewed returning to their burrows (Thursdays only).

Adelaide Visitors Guide, 1978
The cover features the Adelaide Festival Centre. Today this guide would be renamed the Adelaide Brutalist Tour.

Adelaide Day and Half-Day Tours, 1978
The pale peach of the cover is surprisingly restful on the eyes, while the circle and line 'day / half day' device works for me. More importantly, Kangaroo Island does exist.

The South Australian Holiday Planning Guide, 1977
Informative and quite 'racey' publication, complete with a disturbing map featuring big googly eyed travellers.

Sydney, 1976
Detailed booklet covering everything from historical locations to the 'tomorrow look' of the slightly controversial modernist MLC Centre. Great cover utilising a 'zoom' effect with matching typography.

New South Wales, 1973
Lively promotional brochure for NSW, which (didn't you know) could comfortably contain the UK, Germany, Austria, Holland, Denmark and Switzerland combined.

Gippsland Tourist, 1985
This is the free newspaper covering southeastern coastal Australia. I'm not sure it's for me, although there is a musical village in Warragul.

Gippsland
VOLUME 10 NUMBER 2 1985 EDITION
Tourist
FREE
Go where the action is. Go Phillip Island. Go Gippsland.

Seefeld, c.1960s
A pamphlet for the mountainous alpine-plateau health resort, showing the classic illustration style of the period.

Vorarlberg, 1965
I love that the only words in this large fold-out brochure are these four on the front. The rest is just great pictures of snow and fun.

Belgium Camping, 1964
Judging by this extensive triple fold-out map containing hundreds of bustling campsites, Belgium must have been the 1960s camping mecca. It looks like a fine children's book illustrator got the cover gig.

Belgian Coast, 1962
'Easy to reach, impossible to leave!' You have been warned!

PRINTED IN BELGIUM
WEST-VLAANDEREN
Informatie : WESTTOERISME, Brugge (Tel. 050 - 373.78)
Uitgegeven voor WESTTOERISME
door Editions ARTS & VOYAGES, Brussel
Jo MAES - Willy BOSSCHEM

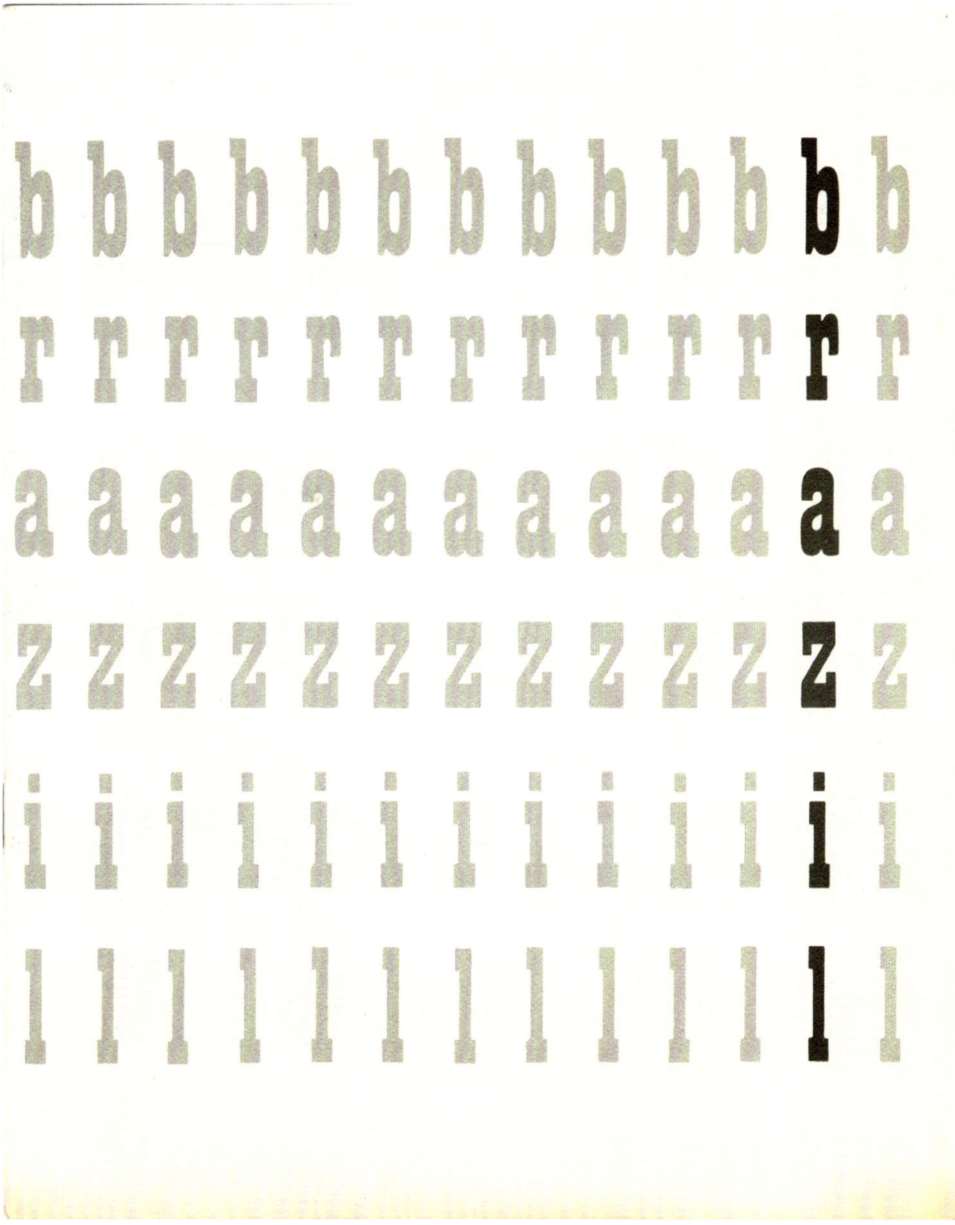

Belgian Coast, late 1950s
This brochure promoting the West Flanders coastal area also has a great internal map produced using the same style as the graphic cover.

Brazil, 1962
Containing pre-bossa nova-era information, this publication boasts more about heavy industry (oil refineries!) than music and culture. Of all the ways of writing 'Brazil', this is the last that would spring to my mind.

Bulgaria, 1968
A charming and naive illustrated A5-size map of Sofia.

Hiking Routes, 1974
Listing comprehensive one-, two- and three-day challenges across the mountains of Rila. Great pictures of snow and fun.

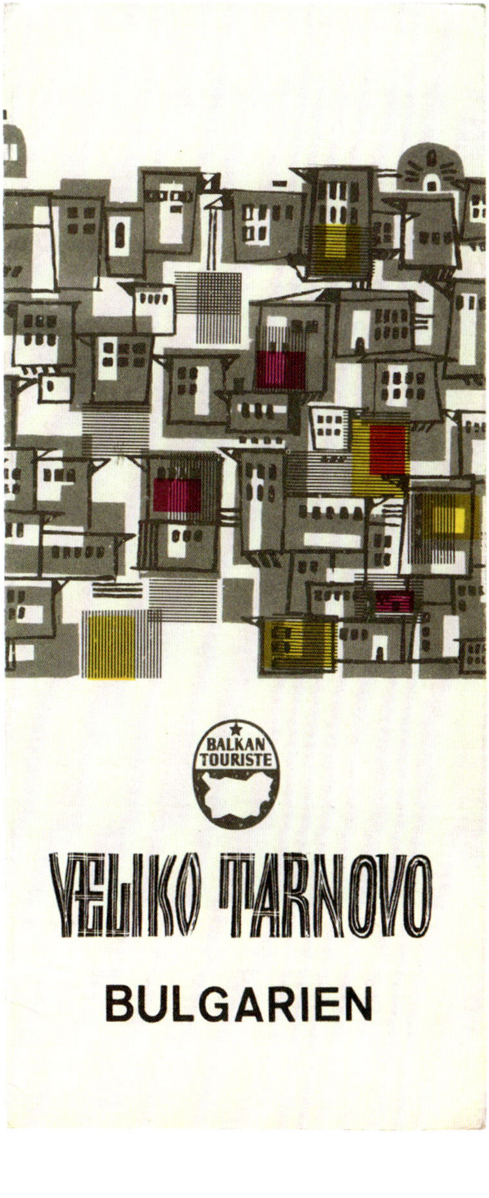

Yelinko Tarnovo, 1967
An illustrated guide to the Bulgarian city.
The only thing written in English – luckily – is the number of the local tourist board.

Bulgaria, early 1960s
A beautiful, undated, driving map and guide.
The title translates as 'Everything for the Motorised Tourist'.

AIR CANADA
ALTA-HUNTING GIBSON
TOURS 69
CANADA
& U.S.A.

Western
Highway
Map
Canada

Air Canada Tours, 1969
This sure seems nonchalant and laid-back, but the approach is justified: flicking through this brochure, Canada appears to have it all.

Western Highway Map, 1974
A very groovy illustration style for this huge fold out. Annoyingly, it lacks any kind of index. Get lost.

Camping Quebec, 1971
A simple fold-out spreadsheet of rustic camp sites and facilities. With a fascinating and unexpected pagan-style illustration.

Fishing in Canada, 1961
An informative and graphically memorable fishing leaflet. I'm hooked.

Trans-Canada Highway, 1958
A brochure covering the 4,497-mile super highway, constructed in the late 1950s.

Go Under Mighty Niagra, 1965
Suitable waterproof fetish wear included with every ticket.

Canadian Cottages, early 1970s
An old-skool bed and breakfast brochure for magnificent Canadian holiday rentals and cabins sleeping up to ten, operated by a small company based in Skipton, North Yorkshire. With a fantastic level of detail on the cover illustration.

Canadian Cottages

INFORMATION
DUBROVNIK
COMPLIMENTARY

Information Dubrovnik, 1973
The unusual oval design is based on the Dubrovnik sailing club pennant, a highly stylised version of the town's coat of arms.

Autocamping Motel, 1962
The sole purpose of this extraordinary leaflet was to direct drivers to the only car-friendly campsite in the country.

Tchécoslovaquie Excursions, 1960
This exciting-looking guide contains a less exciting list of trips for the unsuspecting tourist to endure.

Praha, c.1950s
An undated post-World War II graphic map of Prague. The 'City of a Hundred Spires', a few of which are depicted on the cover.

Le Tourisme en Tchécoslovaquie, 1960
This charming publication from the Czech tourist office contains some fine ink drawings, including one of a Citroën DS.

Tchécoslovaquie, 1963
A brochure citing numerous historical and economic facts. Did you know that in 1961 the country made 162,000 motorbikes and 98 million pairs of shoes?

Bratislava, c.1960s
A castle, a big river and a church with a blue roof. What more could you ask for?

Wonderful Denmark, 1963
The Danish state railway's exceptionally dull guide to holidays in black and white.

Denmark Travel Information, 1962
Containing thoughtfully collated information alongside contact details of important organisations, such as a pen-pal directory.

Egypt, 1950s–1960s
Three Egyptian guides showing a wide range of illustrative styles over a ten-year period. I particularly like the near-collage feel of the Nile Voyage brochure, with its cut-out Temple Arch at Karnak and symbol-like white dahabiya sailing by.

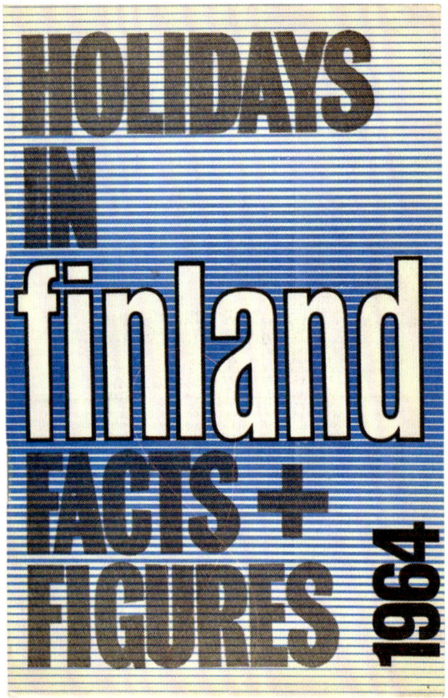

Holidays In Finland Facts + Figures, 1964
'Made for the British holiday maker, this brochure allows him to travel widely and choose his favourite form of relaxation.' A brochure aimed squarely at the male tourist.

The Finnish Connection, 1979
A beautifully printed and very persuasive brochure. The black and white photographs are reproduced using silver ink, so the sea twinkles and the snow glistens. Genius.

Welcome to Jyväskylä, c1960s
Tourist activities include visits to woodlands, metal factories, beach excursions and car rallying (something the 'Flying Finns' were particularly famous for).

Tehi
JY
VÄS
KYLÄ
THE MIDDLE POINT IN FINLAND

The Key for Your Trip to France, c.1950s
With a text by the French government that spells out the six faces of faultless travel: F=Fascination, R=Relaxation, A=Amusement, N=Novelty, C=Comparison, E= Education. Can we add Q=Questionable?

Camping in France, 1960
I reckon they put a cockerel on the front because he'll be waking you up at the crack of dawn every morning, without fail. Wherever you camp in France. Even in 1960.

Monte Carlo, c.1965
This glamorous freebie includes a map detailing notable locations of the tax-free enclave. Very professional oily artwork.

The Seaside of France, c.1959
A very concise guide to every beach in France. With easy to follow keys to beach type (sand, shingle, etc.) as well as the number of casinos, tennis courts, hotels, rooms and more.

France Motoring, 1965
This colourful aid to 436,000 miles of French roads features some brilliant and energetic animation-style drawings.

Choose the Nievre, 1967
Presenting alphabetical assistance for the French tourist visiting the area, including valuable information on fishing, camping and *naturellement*, chateaus.

France by Train and Ship, 1971
Containing simple and well-conceived timetables for rail and ferries from the UK to mainland France and beyond. Genius idea to use the map as a torso.

SNCF
France
2
VOITURE
27

French Railways

France SNCF, c.1970s
Just two examples of the many well-art-directed timetables and information booklets from the National Company of French Railways (SNCF). Possibly created in-house, as there is no indication as to who the designers were.

Shell Berre, c.1960s
There is something oddly romantic about a night-time map showing the exact location of every 24-hour garage in France. Even though some only appear to open at intermittent times.

Paris Tour Eiffel, late 1960s
Great use of the perfect tree. I'm tempted to go and find it now and see if it still matches up.

Bienvenue à Paris, c.1970s
This classy, complimentary guide, was produced by the historic superstore that still is Galeries Lafayette.

Black Forest – Lake Constance, late 1950s
An impressive, vibrant map and information guide to Germany's 'largest medium-altitude range'. Great use of colour blocks and screen washes.

Always in Good Hands in Bonn, 1962
A scramble of times, numbers, letters and spreadsheets. One for the enthusiast or brave traveller with a maths degree. Fine, straightforward illustration on the cover.

The North of Germany, 1972
A West German Federal Railway (Deutsche Bundesbahn, or DB) fold-out brochure, that mixes cartoons with collage and gets away with it. With a really unusual collage on the cover to grab everyone's attention.

Berlin is Worth a Trip, 1964
These off-kilter graphics mess with the typesetting and crop off part of the circle, taking conceivably dull material and making it a little more engaging.

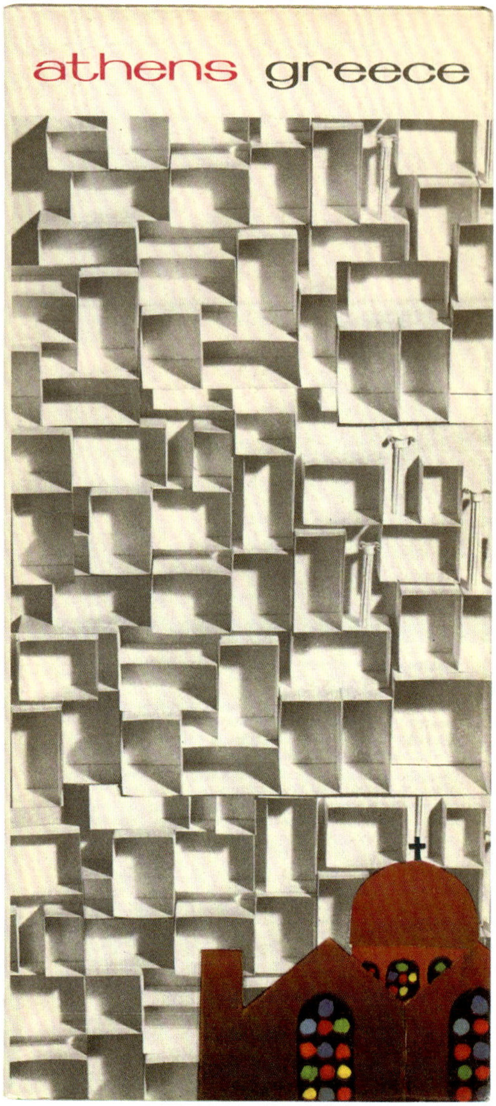

Chandris Cruises, 1966
This is a very black and orange introduction to the SS *Fantasia*, air-conditioned queen of the Aegean.

Athens Greece, 1967
The fold-out map inside this brochure uses Ionic columns as a graphic device and just about gets away with it.

Greece / Athens, 1962
With a strong educational bent this leaflet, containing a map and information, has sections dedicated to myths and antiquities as well as all the museum opening times. A nicely illustrated cover in period style.

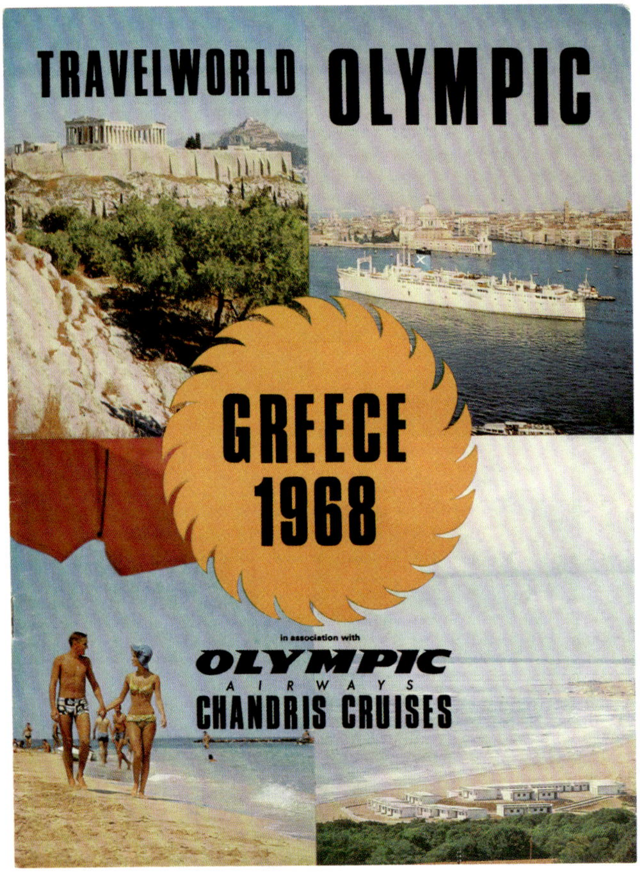

Travelworld Olympic Greece, 1968
Offering you both ancient and utterly modern holiday experiences to Greece and the islands, via a luxury liner and a hotel that is ominously 'nearing completion'.

Typaldos Lines Greece, 1968
This brochure offers you the opportunity to 'sail with the sun', on a ship called *Mykonos*, complete with onboard nightclub. Don't forget to pack your sea legs.

Typaldos Lines Cruises, 1965
I quite fancy the Easter Pharaonic cruise. From Venice to Athens and back over a long hot week with my graphic suitcase.

Greece
Israel
Turkey
Egypt
Lebanon
Canary Islands
Black Sea
Spring- and Easter-Time Cruises
1965
TYPALDOS LINES

Hawaii, 1974
A brochure from a series exploring the verdant group of islands, issued by the Hawaii Visitors Bureau.

Hawaiian Volcanoes, 1974
This leaflet reported road closures due to recent lava flows from the Kīlauea volcano. The dynamic angry red paint cover is simple but powerfully effective.

Holland, c.1960s
This charming early British brochure sells this 'flat and fertile' country very well.

Holland Facts and Information, c.1960s
This brochure contains one of the more unusual maps, showing towns listed according to bed capacity. The design, with its arrows pointing in different directions, symbols and block colours, keeps me trying to understand the concept behind it.

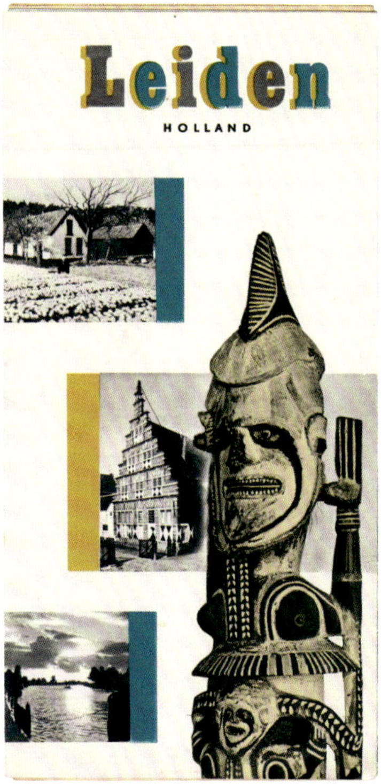

Gouda, c.1970
Featuring some strong cheese graphics, this is the only cheese brochure in this book. According to the information inside, Gouda is only sold between 9am and 10am, from May to September.

Leiden, c.1960s
This town, built on an artificial hill, is the birthplace of Rembrandt. It's full of culture, as you can tell from this small leaflet.

Welcome in Venlo, 1965
One of the greenest cities in Europe. Another outstanding feature is the 'the good-natured kindliness of its inhabitants'.

Amsterdam Evening Tour, 1967
A night out on the town including a visit to the 'gayest Weinstube' (traditional tavern), and a nightclub called 'Extase' (cloakroom fees not included). I'm in.

Rotterdam Sightseeing, 1965
This groovy-looking leaflet contains a wholly uninspiring list of highlights from 'the city of tomorrow', such as new 12-storey blocks of flats and traffic squares. I'm not sure what that random arrow is doing on the cover.

Hungary Hotel Guide, 1964
Not really a guide, more a pocket-sized, origami-style, double fold-out map of hotel and campsite locations. Front and back of brochure shown here.

Camping Hungary, c.1962
My favourite thing in this leaflet is the map legend, including oddities such as: fruit-bearing garden, espresso, isolated cave and railway station with shelter. Everything you need really. A fine rustic-style design on the front too.

CAMPING
UNGARN
HONGRIE HUNGARY
ВЕНГРИЯ

Iceland, 1970
Tourist Bureau information showing all the usual geysers and knitwear. It also includes the futuristic Kopavogur Church which looks like something from a *Star Wars* set.

Road Map of India, c.1970s
You'll need all the space on the bus just to unfold this massive travellers' map. Then you'd really struggle to fold it all back up again. Wouldn't it be great if the roads in India were actually pink?

ROAD MAP
OF INDIA
SURVEY OF INDIA
1767
भारत का
सड़क मानचित्र
मूल्य: रू० 45.00
Price: Rs.
1:2,500,000

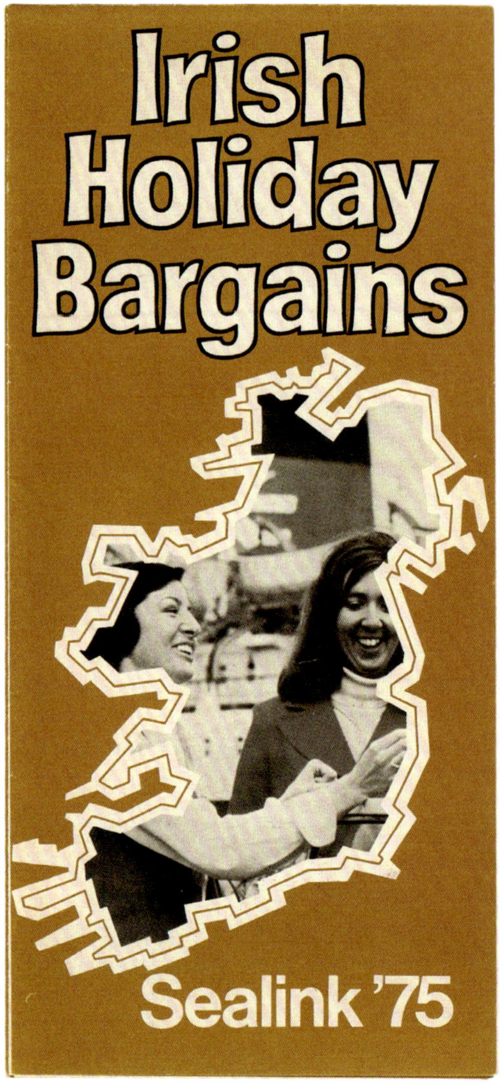

Ireland, c.1968
A folky and poetic fold out. This heavily illustrated guide has a lively text by the acclaimed short-story writer Sean O'Faolain (1900–1991), so it's more of a yarn than a tourist listing.

Sealink Irish Holiday Bargains, 1975
Packed with ferry deals for the budget traveller. Nice use of the classic cut-out device for full (but economic) design impact.

Strand Hotel, 1962
The well-stocked Lounge Bar is said to be the most pleasant 'in all Ireland'. Also on offer are the contrasting activities of birdwatching and shooting wild fowl.

Ireland International Hotel Killarney, 1970
Quite a striking, modern leaflet design for a hotel that is really nothing like that.

Siena, 1976
I knew nothing of the sacred wafers miracle of 1730 (a Catholic event where consecrated wafers turn into human flesh) until I found this small brochure. I can feel a pilgrimage coming on.

Hotel Margutta, c.1962
Not overly inspiring, hopefully it looks a lot better than this in real life.

Rome, New Illustrated Guide, 1954
This guide, with its fantastic modernist cover type, contains not only everything you need in terms of day- and night-time activities, but also superb reproductions of the city's most important works of art.

Alitalia Airlines, 1968
Promoting their fabulous 16-day 'Red Car' first-class trips to Italy. I've always been a fan of this 1960s two-colour, Ken Garland style of graphic treatment. Is it me or is the woman getting out of the car a bit short?

SUMMER
HOLIDAYS
1963
ITALY
ITALIAN TRAVEL SERVICE
69, EBURY STREET, LONDON, S.W.1. TEL. SLO 9914

Summer Holidays Italy, 1963
The Swiss Travel Service extended its operations to Italy as the desire for exotic, post-war travel rapidly expanded. Love the clever block-colour artwork.

Pompei Plan, 1955
They sure knew how to make a plan of Pompeii look good back then. Really great hand-painted illustration and lettering.

Roman Soujourn, 1968
I do love a confident, simplified graphic illustration, even more if the subject matter is a Wonder of the World like this one.

Hotel La Residenza Capri, c.1970
A hotel set on the fertile hillside of the island, where the volcanic ash from Vesuvius once fell. It's still open!

Siracusa, 1974
If you turned up in Syracuse in the 1970s you'd be gifted this free map showing seven different routes around the region and pinpointing 70 miles of sexy beaches.

Riviera dei Fiori, 1972
If you were hitting the Italian Riviera in the early 1970s there were hundreds of hotels, campsites and bungalows to choose from, and this booklet lists them all, sadly without any pictures. But the illustration on the front is really quite something, bold and a bit odd. I'd definitely pick it up.

Isola d'Elba, c.1970s
Chunky, paired-back, 'fat pen' cover design, which I like a lot. However, nothing about Napoleon (who was exiled to the island in 1814) and just one paragraph about how to get there. Little else apart from photographs. It's almost as if they don't want you there, and I get that.

3 Tropical Island Holidays, 1957
'So near yet so delightfully foreign!' Jamaica, Nassau and Bermuda looking exciting and exotic, 'full of scenic beauty and native rhythms'.

It's 'Tee-Time' in Jamaica, 1964
An illustrated leaflet aimed at American golfers. Eight courses await you for perpetual play.

Cooks Holidays in the Bahamas, 1967
16 days in paradise including transfers for just £155.

Jamaica Water Sports, 1972
This cover makes full use of the legendary, closely kerned, 'Jamaica' logo. Created by the Doyle Dane Bernbach agency, their tourism campaign was a huge success, that revolutionised holiday advertising.

Jamaica, c.1950
An early tourist brochure for 'the most beautiful island in the world'. Flights from London took a mere 26 hours.

Hotel New Hiroshima, c.1960s
A pioneering symbol of the city's post-war regeneration, this hotel was established in 1950 and features in Alain Resnais' classic romance *Hiroshima Mon Amour* (1959).

Hotel New Hiroshima
新広島ホテル
Hotel
New Hiroshima

The Japan of Today, 1967
A Ministry of Foreign Affairs booklet that contains import and export figures alongside tourism suggestions.

British Airways Japan, 1974
This small but surprisingly informative leaflet also includes pocket calculator and tape recorder advertisements.

Panorama 36, 1969
A booklet for the tallest skyscraper in Tokyo (at the time), the 36-storey Kasumigaseki Building, which was completed in 1968. It has a view of the National Diet Building from the top. Really groovy hand-drawn graphics and typography.

PANORAMA 36
360度——東京を空から見おろす
霞が関ビル展望台
パノラマ36

HOBBIES, SPORTS & RECREATION OF JAPAN
TRADITIONAL SPORTS
JAPAN AIR LINES

THE CULTURE OF JAPAN
THE TEA CEREMONY
JAPAN AIR LINES

THE CULTURE OF JAPAN
ESTHETICS
JAPAN AIR LINES

HISTORY & GEOGRAPHY
HISTORY OF JAPAN
JAPAN AIR LINES

THE CULTURE OF JAPAN
FLOWER ARRANGING
JAPAN AIR LINES

THE CULTURE OF JAPAN
CERAMIC ARTS
JAPAN AIR LINES

Japan Air Lines, 1965
Elegant, graphically refined, information leaflets utilising well-drawn simplifications of everyday Japanese subject matter.

Your Passport to Fun in Mexico!, 1969
Easily digestible information about what (and what not) to do. No mention of cartels.

Mexico As-U-Like-It, 1969
Note the lovely graphic bull. I'm not sure who Mr Foster is, but he tells us all about fiestas, pyramids and bullfights.

U-Plan-It Mexico, 1965
If only all holiday planners had followed this painless format – you simply choose your options and tick them with a pencil to book. It's no big jigsaw puzzle.

Excursions in Morocco, c.1970s
A tourist guide offering everything from trips for history buffs to treks in the high Atlas mountain range.

Morocco Awaits You, 1970
Despite its cartoonish exterior, this leaflet contains some interesting and essential tourist information.

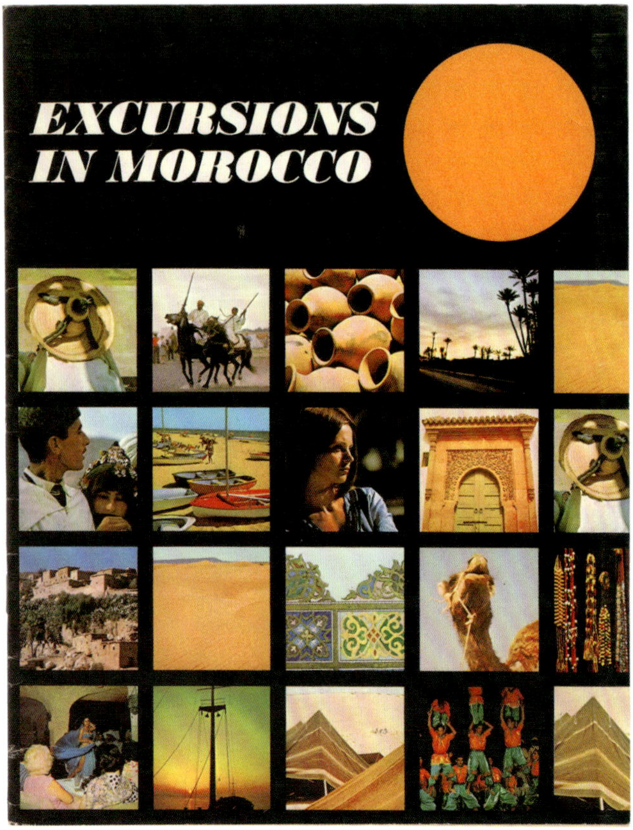

MOROCCO
AWAITS
YOU

NEW ZEALAND

New Zealand, 1958
I've only just realised that this cover is actually a cunning collage.

New Zealand Is a Must!, c.1962
Good news! This leaflet advises the traveller that the country has no snakes, poisonous insects or dangerous wild animals.

See You In... New Zealand, c.1965
Yes, see you there, and we can all visit the Waitomo Glowworm Caves.

Fly NAC, c.1968
Produced by the New Zealand Airways Corporation (NAC). This domestic airline offers aircraft services all over the country and snow planes (fitted with ski landing gear) in the mountains.

Holidays in Norway, 1951
A guide to 'nature's wonderland' with the warmest summer seas in Europe. That's news to me.

Norway by Car, 1976
You could take this map with all its copious information and really get stuck into a road-based break. Although these days you'd probably be in a hideous queue of social media personalities to get where that woman is standing (the famous viewpoint and gorge of Flydalsjuvet).

Norway Winter Sports Holiday, 1956
Giving details for popular resorts across the mountains of Norway. Interestingly all these skiing breaks could be booked through the Youth Hostels Association (YHA) in the UK.

Norway Winters Sports, 1965
Lively holidays on a variety of slopes, perfect for the 'piste basher'.

Bergen Line 1968
Includes 'ski-touring' holiday offers, going from one mountain hut to another – seems like more of an endurance test than holiday. This is the best graphic use of a ski glove I've come across.

NORWAY
BY BERGEN LINE
WINTER SPORTS
HOLIDAYS
1956-57

ski-ing holidays in Norway
by Bergen Line 1968/9
ski-ing, ski touring

NORWAY
WINTER SPORTS
1965/66

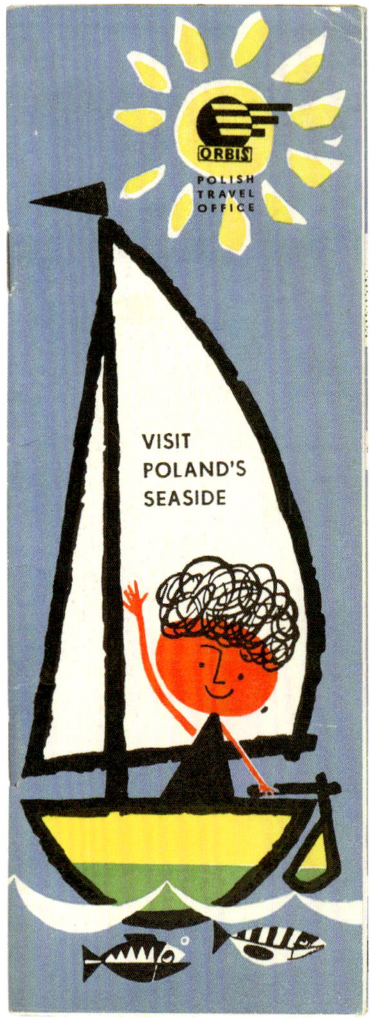

Holidays in Poland, 1957
This Orbis travel brochure offers sun, sea, spas and ski jumping.

Visit Poland's Seaside, c.1958
Explore 300 miles of spectacular coastline, creatively summed up in a brochure that's only 4 centimetres wide.

By Car Through Poland to the USSR, c.1960
An engaging naive graphic style. If you taske one thing from this brochure, it should be that 'horning' is forbidden in towns.

VISIT POLAND!
BY CAR
THROUGH
POLAND
TO THE U.S.S.R.

Hotel da Baleeira, c.1970
The only reason this is in here is because it's such an odd and impractical shape. Which I find a bit triggering.

Your Visit to Portugal, 1970
This unusual leaflet with it's bold black, white and orange colour scheme could have easily been inspired by the Sainsbury's Own Label design book.

Regular Tours and Sightseeing, 1967
Plenty of entertaining tours available here: Artistic Lisbon, Old Lisbon, Typical Lisbon at Night, or the slightly more daring Cosmopolitan Lisbon at Night.

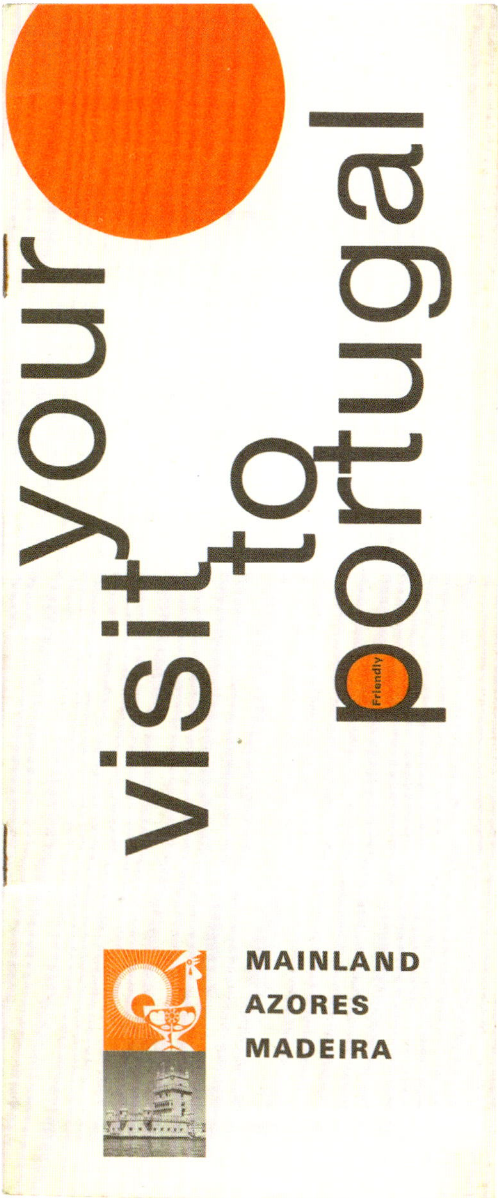
your visit to portugal
Friendly
MAINLAND
AZORES
MADEIRA

REGULAR TOURS AND SIGHTSEEING IN
PORTUGAL
1967
STAR
TRAVEL
TOURISM

Madeira, 1973
Could this woman be representing the Madeira Carnival in February? Or the Flower Festival in April? Or the Grape Harvest Festival in September? She might be a fixture at all of them. Note the unusual, perfectly picked, flower font.

Come to Lisbon in Winter, 1960s
An unusual brochure trying to lure tourists to Lisbon simply through photography and poetry from the likes of Wordsworth, Longfellow, Tennyson, etc. Madness.

Portugal, 1967
One brochure giving us just two options – Lisbon or the countryside. As simple as that.

Romania Histria, c.1964
Welcome to the 'Romanian Pompeii'.

Soyez les Bienvenus en Roumanie, 1963
Welcome to Romania's colourful and abundant mountains and lakes.

Rumania Mamaia, c.1958
This is the best map ever, simply a very long, slim fold out, detailing an 8 kilometre by 300 metre strip of beachy land.

„CARPAŢI" NATIONAL TRAVEL OFFICE
RUMANIA
mamaia

Firestone Hispania Maps, c.1970s
An interesting, slightly wacky, combination of maps and illustration. Good to see some effort went into these; they certainly look more interesting than the usual versions.

Benidorm Wings, 1965
A rare brochure for the first wave of modern package-holiday hotels, built in what was originally a small and quiet fishing village.

BENIDORM
WINGS 1965
Don Everall Travel Ltd.
The Travel Centre,,

Vernon Holidays, 1968
An unusually restrained and first-classy brochure. We don't want girls in bikinis, beach scenes, or any novelty here. There is a whiff of 'jazz' about the style of this design.

Camping Caravaning Barcelona, c.1967
This campsite, just 15 kilometres from the city, has every modern convenience you could wish for (and more), if you were forced to be in a tent.

Gibraltar, c.1960s
'Feel free in friendly Gib' appears to be part of a campaign that included Alfredo the Ape (Barbary macaques being a famous symbol of the British Overseas Territory).

Hotel Gran Tinerfe, 1972
The first brochure for this pioneering, beachfront high-rise hotel in the Playa de las Americas, heralding the dawn of mass tourism to the area.

APAL, 1968
Here we are, back to basics with girls in bikinis, as well as a bewildering array of package deals.

SCANDINAVIAN HOLIDAYS
1961
LAMBERT BROTHERS LTD : VIKING TOURS

SWEDEN
New Budget Holidays
by ENGLAND SWEDEN LINE

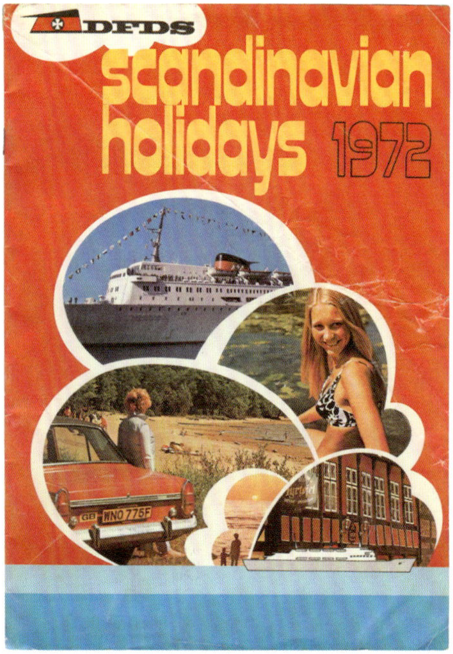
DFDS
scandinavian
holidays 1972

Scandinavian Holidays, 1961
My heart skips a beat when I see such fine stained-glass-style illustration. This was for the appropriately titled Viking Tours, London E3, who were bringing you the best in newly built, brutalist holiday accommodation.

Sweden New Budget Holidays, 1969
Early budget excursions by Thomas Cook to Sweden, via boat in a claustrophobic cabin. It appears they stuck to a low budget with this cover by making a doll from a toilet roll.

Scandinavian Holidays, 1972
A cheerful, colourful brochure, containing some exciting offerings including Summer Bungalows, Farmhouse Holidays and 'Buy Denmark for £8'.

Eskilstuna, 1962
Groovy brochure for the '12th biggest town in Sweden'. Monkeys on ladders are a recurring motif, representing the upward mobility of local workers and industrial progress. Not what I was expecting.

The Mushroom Water-tower at Örebro, Sweden lies on E3 and E 18
Let The Mushroom
be the 'high-point'
of your day!

The Mushroom, 1966
A brochure for the Orebro water-tower. Climb the mushroom and see the sights while standing on top of 9,000 cubic metres of water.

Sweden in Summer-Time, c.1962
Have you ever experienced an 'Archipelago summer'? I haven't, but with the amount of spas and sanitoriums listed here I'm certainly tempted.

Customs Control Brochure, c.1965
Superb spare graphics for harsh Swedish customs control regulations. All the booze, fags and firearms information you need, for red or green light travel, can be found here.

MONTREUX-VEVEY
Holidays
on the Swiss Riviera
Railways and boats
TIME-TABLE
FARES
1949

Holidays
in
Switzerland
by rail and alpine postal motor-coach

Holidays on the Swiss Riviera, 1949
An impressive, loose, blobby graphic vibe for this prescient brochure, the earliest in the book. Just superb.

Holidays in Switzerland, 1961
Including organised travel by postal motorcoach – yellow coaches run by the Swiss Postal Administration.

The New Rhine Cruise, 1960
Beautiful brochure for cruising on the MS *Europa*. A ship full of 'congenial people' with no subdivision of classes.

Jungfrau / Jungfrau, c.1965
Welcome to the top of Europe. A place of ice palaces, polar dogs and a 'Sphinx Tunnel' that houses a lift transporting you directly from the railway station to the Observatory, 3,571 metres above sea level. Coffee on the terrace with a bird when you're back.

Grindelwald, c.1965
An ideal holiday spot for the rambler – with extensive path networks, fragrant woods and dramatic gorges.

Mürren, c.1965
More alpine wonders to look at, a mere 20 hours by train from London.

Lake Thun, c.1950s
Popular alpine holiday lake. Nothing in this lovely brochure mentions the Swiss government dumped their unused munitions at the bottom.

Lausanne, 1949
At the time this was the perfect destination for a 'cosmopolitan rendezvous'.

Grindelwald
SCHWEIZ SUISSE SWITZERLAND

LAKE OF THUN
BERNESE OBERLAND SWITZERLAND

MÜRREN
5450 ft.
Berner Oberland Oberland Bernois Bernese Oberland
1650 m Schweiz Suisse Switzerland

Lausanne
FRENCH SWITZERLAND
THE GOLDEN YEAR THROUGH

Swiss Chalets, 1973
This comprehensive, mind-boggling directory of chalets, apartments and flats located across the Alps, contains no interior photographs or ratings to help you choose.

Regional Season Ticket Brochure, 1972
Unlimited travel for 7 or 15 days. Children and dogs also require tickets; these are priced at half the full fare.

Zermatt, 1957 / Zermatt, 1958
Early guides to this winter wonderland situated 5,310 ft above sea level. Surprisingly adventurous graphics for the time – grids, crosses and a simple use of colour creating truly modern styles.

Bursa and Environs, c.1970
Quite an unconventional guide to the area, featuring incongruous photographs of a chair lift, carpet weaving and some peaches in a bowl.

Turkey, East Anatolia, c.1960s
A modernist guide to ancient attractions.

Spot on In Istanbul, 1960s
Curious, counter-culture-style fold out, involving collage, illustration and idiosyncratic design. Unusual to have gambling, sex and pleasure listed so blatantly. A powerful graphic style, the biggest finger in the book for sure.

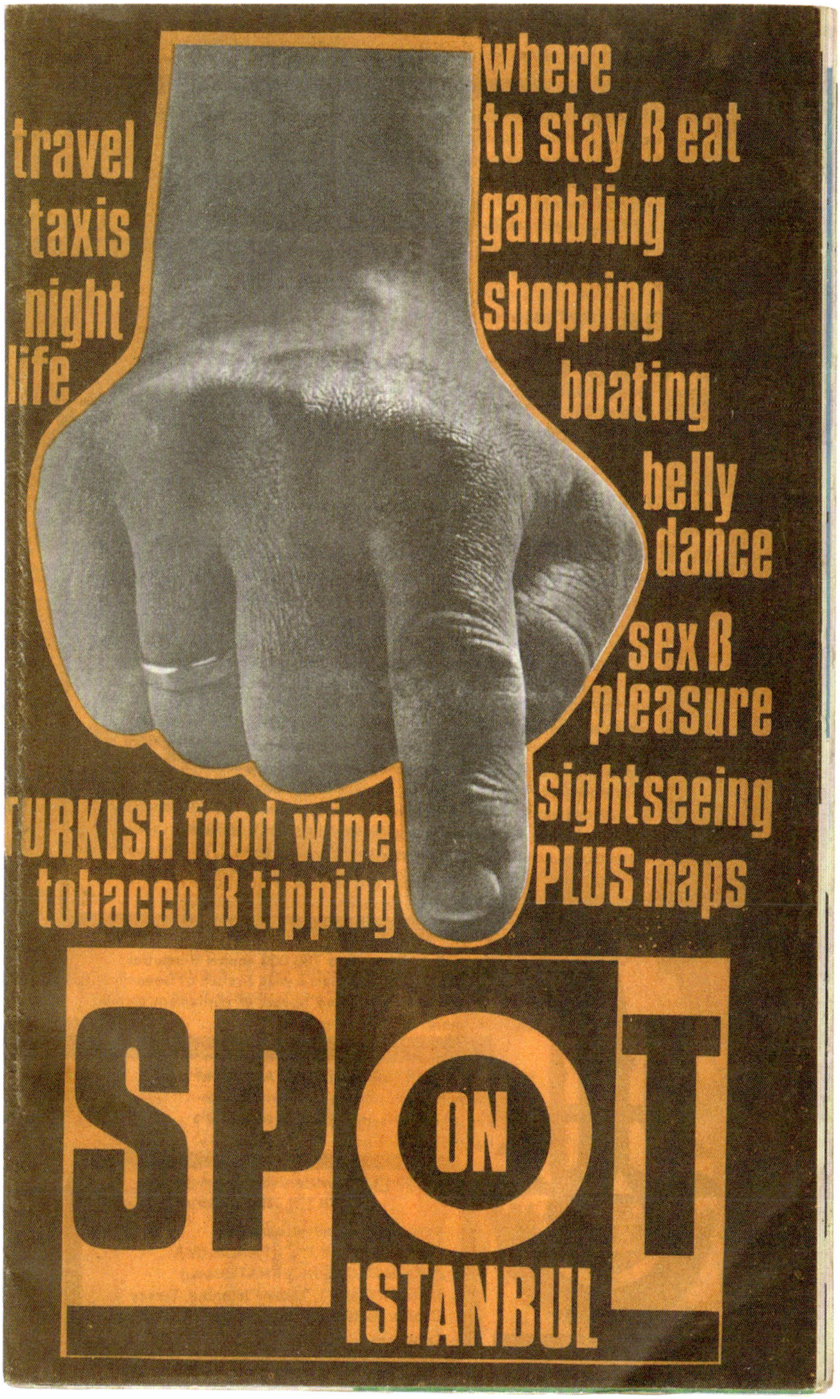
travel
taxis
night
life
where
to stay & eat
gambling
shopping
boating
belly
dance
sex &
pleasure
sightseeing
PLUS maps
TURKISH food wine
tobacco & tipping
SPOT
ON
ISTANBUL

Jersey Holiday Brochures, 1960s
I've got the feeling that Hills of Jersey pretty much owned tourism there, employing local talent for all their brochure artwork.

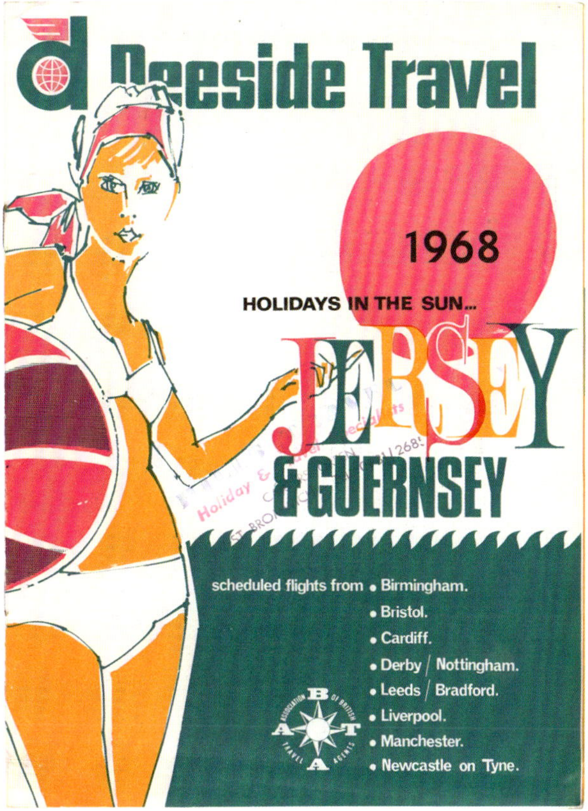
Deeside Travel
1968
HOLIDAYS IN THE SUN...
JERSEY
& GUERNSEY
scheduled flights from
• Birmingham.
• Bristol.
• Cardiff.
• Derby / Nottingham.
• Leeds / Bradford.
• Liverpool.
• Manchester.
• Newcastle on Tyne.

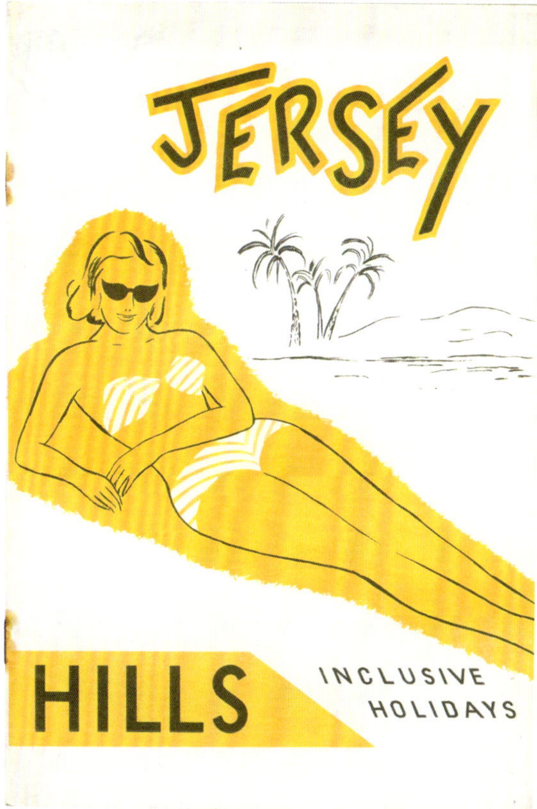
JERSEY
HILLS
INCLUSIVE
HOLIDAYS

P&O
around the world with P&O around the world with P&O around the world with P&O

Sealink
Continent, Ireland, Channel Islands, Isle of Wight
MOTORWAY EUROPE
Ro
Sealink
ro
Sealink is the brand name for the shipping fleets of British Rail, French Railways, Belgian Maritime Transport Authority, Dutch Zeeland Steamship Co.
Freight Sales Department, Eversholt House, Eversholt Street, London NW1 1BG, Telephone 01-387 1234

ENGLAND
OSLO
NEWCASTLE -
via Kristiansand
vinter
1967/68
Fred.Olsen Lines

SUNSHINE CRUISING with FRAMES' 1964/65

Around the World with P&O, 1969
Ten fine ships, one fine brochure. Taking you anywhere you want to go, via obvious but efficient cover graphics.

Sealink Motorway Europe, 1975

England Oslo-Newcastle, 1967
Perhaps not the most romantic of routes.

Sunshine Cruising with Frames, 1964
Includes 99-day around-the-world tours from as little as £383.

Crusie Chandris, 1978
Wherever we're going I'm in!

Leisure, Pleasure, Sun, Fun, 1973
A five-port trip from Southampton to Lagos on the *Aureol*. This passenger liner has a tobacconist shop on board.

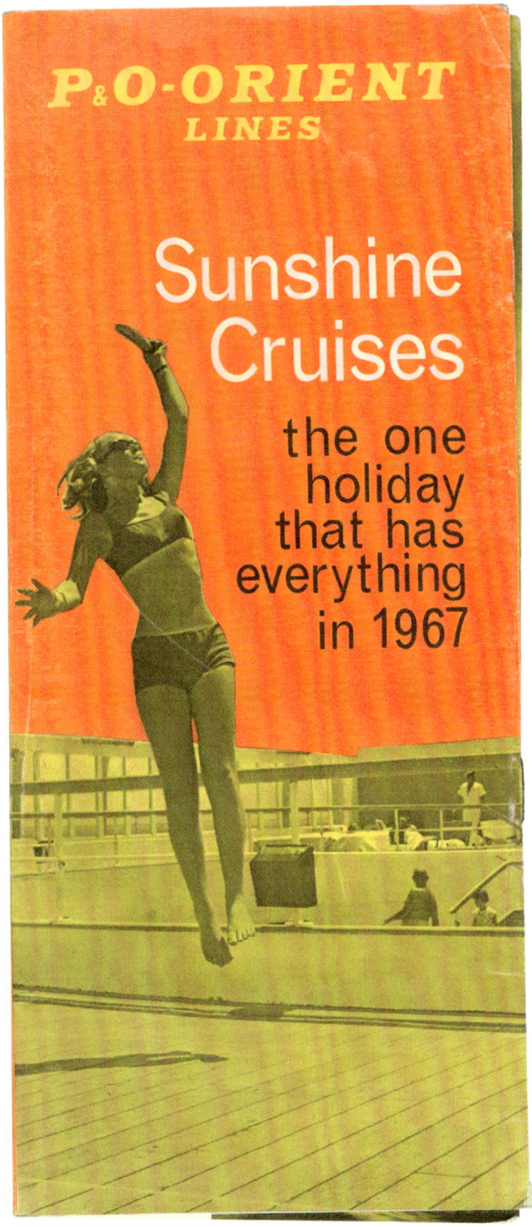
P&O-ORIENT
LINES
Sunshine
Cruises
the one
holiday
that has
everything
in 1967

The SHORT sea route
between Britain and
Northern Ireland
via STRANRAER
and LARNE
70 MINUTES OPEN SEA PASSAGE
Passenger
and car ferry
service
4th June to
10th September
1960
BRITISH RAILWAYS

P&O Orient Lines Sunshine Cruises, 1967
A fleet of seven 'great white' liners for 32 organised cruises, shipping you to the sun and back, in style and luxury. Great 1960s colour scheme and visual treatment.

The Short Sea Route, 1960
Nothing more than a train and steamer timetable between Scotland and Ireland, but nice to see that the illustrator enjoyed themselves on the way.

British Rail / Sealink Ticket Holder, 1970
A lovely, die-cut logo ticket holder, for your rail journey and sea cruise tickets.

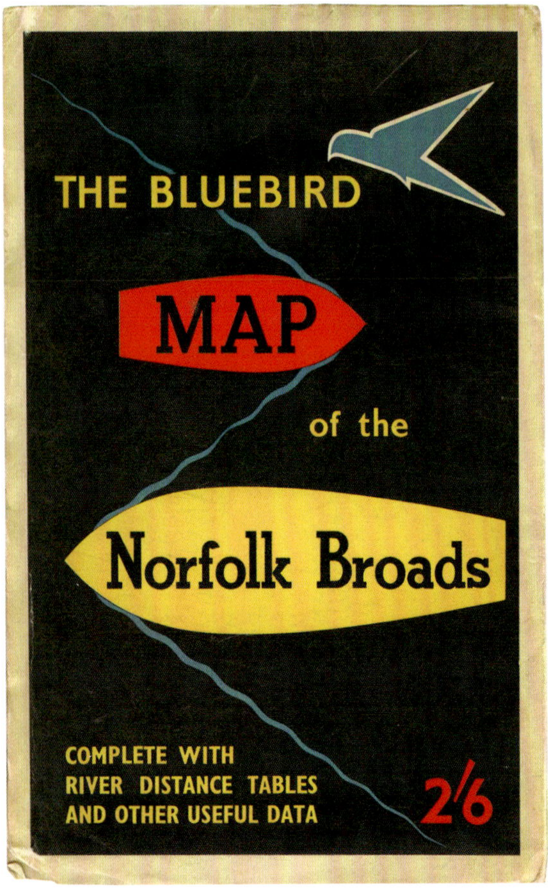

See More of Windermere, 1973
The timetable and prices for the Sealink Ferry across Windermere. Hopefully missing United Utilities' latest sewage dump. Superb colours and a classic 1930s feel.

Holidays Afloat, 1966
A brochure for boat hire and holidays on the Fenland Waterways. £20 bought you a week plus a full tank of fuel. Brilliantly simple graphics show the various types of craft.

Bluebird Map of the Norfolk Broads, 1960s
This map of the Broads contains priceless information for holiday makers, including early closing days for every Norfolk village.

Holidays on Inland Waterways, 1966
All you need to find, hire and navigate the perfect holiday afloat on the Norfolk Broads.

SEE MORE OF WINDERMERE
...with Sealink
Fares and Services 1973

HOLIDAYS AFLOAT
ON THE FENLAND WATERWAYS 1966
Appleyard, Lincoln & Co Ltd

Post House Epping, 1970
With 60 bedrooms, central heating and an open-air car park.

Post House Norwich, 1970
Just 2 miles from Norwich. Very suitable for businessmen. Carmen hair rollers and Ronson razors available.

Hotels Motels, 1970
The design of this leaflet is a graphic delight, somewhere between Mexican (typeface) and municipal (directional arrow).

King Malcolm Hotel, 1970
I've no idea who King Malcolm is, but they named a hotel in Dunfermline after him. The premises encompasses the Canmore Lounge, with vaulted ceiling and murals.

London Norfolk Hotel, 1960s
A very cool two-colour leaflet for a boutique hotel in South Kensington. Today it's called the Ampersand Hotel. The '&' apparently connects its guests to the best of the area. The Norfolk's groovy, padded, bench-meets-chandelier, restaurant seating will be long gone.

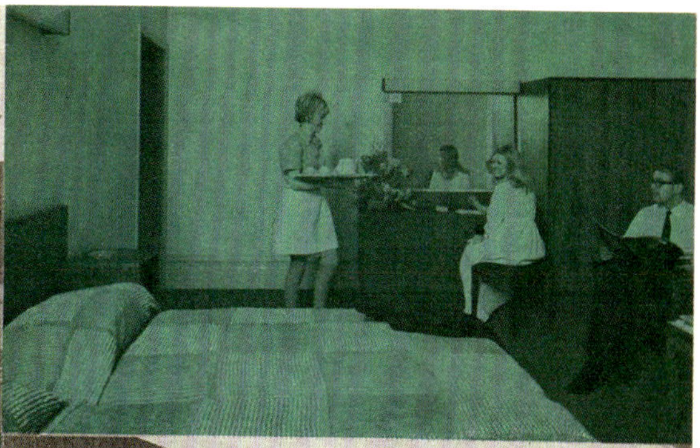

PINDISPORTS
CATALOGUE
1970

Pindisports Catalogue, 1970
I love the bold outline font, used to great effect here, but the real highlight has to be the polywarm sleeping bags featured on page 16. The factory manufacture process takes just one minute from start to finish and uses only the finest man-made fibres.

Pindisports Catalogue, 1959
An early, comprehensive mail-order catalogue of progressive camping equipment. They were the first company to offer framed tents and 'swell' dehydrated vegetables. Yum.

Camping & Outdoor Activities, 1973
This catalogue, issued by the Scout Association, captures a moment in time. Of course, I headed straight to the clothing section, where I drooled over odd gorpcore things such as 'the Cagjac', a garment that combines the best aspects of the cagoule and the casual jacket. At last.

Canvas Holidays, 1973
Offering European sunshine and large modern framed tents. Like the ones (rarely) won on game shows back then.

The AA Camping and Caravan Guides, 1960s
These annual comprehensive directories to pan-European camping were all set in the most unhelpful tiny font.

AUTRICHE AUSTRIA
ÖSTERREICH
HONGRIE HUNGARY
MAGYARORSZÁG
TCHÉCOSLOVAQUIE
ČESKOSLOVENSKO
CAMPING
CARAVANNING
GUIDE
1966/67
Published by
Centre de documentation camping-caravaning de l'A.I.T., Geneva
for
THE AUTOMOBILE ASSOCIATION
Fanum House, Leicester Square
LONDON W.C. 2
AA
AIT

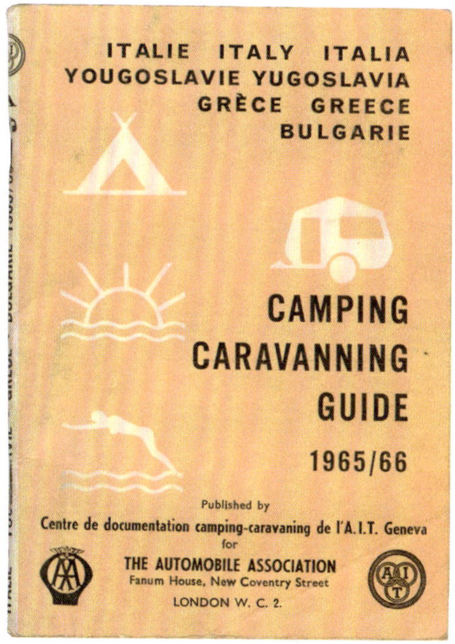
ITALIE ITALY ITALIA
YOUGOSLAVIE YUGOSLAVIA
GRÈCE GREECE
BULGARIE
CAMPING
CARAVANNING
GUIDE
1965/66
Published by
Centre de documentation camping-caravaning de l'A.I.T. Geneva
for
THE AUTOMOBILE ASSOCIATION
Fanum House, New Coventry Street
LONDON W. C. 2.
AIT

ALLEMAGNE GERMANY
DEUTSCHLAND
POLOGNE POLAND
POLSKA
CAMPING
CARAVANNING
GUIDE
1966/67
Published by
Centre de documentation camping-caravaning de l'A.I.T., Geneva
for
THE AUTOMOBILE ASSOCIATION
Fanum House, Leicester Square
LONDON W.C. 2
AA
AIT

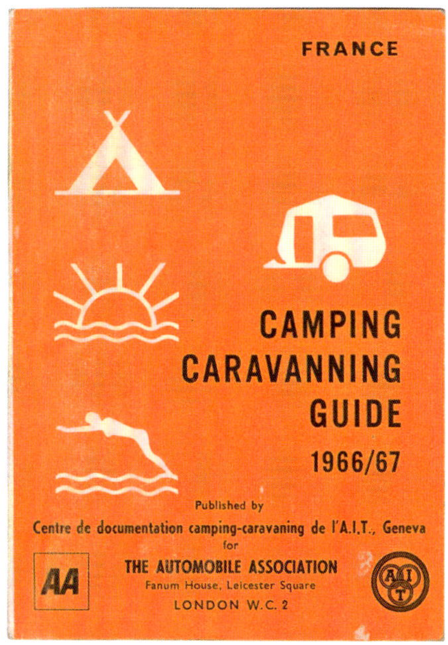
FRANCE
CAMPING
CARAVANNING
GUIDE
1966/67
Published by
Centre de documentation camping-caravaning de l'A.I.T., Geneva
for
THE AUTOMOBILE ASSOCIATION
Fanum House, Leicester Square
LONDON W.C. 2
AA
AIT

Autoplan, 1967
Truly exciting European opportunities for the keen British motorist, all graphically illustrated using popular British car silhouettes: MGs, Jaguars, Austins, Minis and Triumph Heralds.

Rent-A-Car, 1975
From E&P in Sloane Avenue, SW3. Self-drive car hire from £4.25 a day for a Mini and £6.75 for a Capri 1600. Perfect low-budget graphics for low-budget car rental.

Cooks Holidays for the Motorist, 1962
The chance to drive across Europe – crossing the Channel via ferry or 'Sky Bridge' (nose-loading aircraft). It looks like this guy went all on his own.

Drive Your Own Car, 1970
This unusual, eye-catching illustration of the car, family and the sun, could well be the most joyous bit of the whole holiday.

The Lights Are Green All The Way, 1976
A charming, slightly hippie feel to this second 'drive-your-own-car' holiday brochure. This one includes a guide in five languages and a sweet little checklist, every item of which has been ticked off.

Florence & Grange Tours, 1962
Exciting offerings including a 5-day 'Christmas Tour to Torquay', and 'The Battle of the Flowers', a 14-day trip covering the French and Italian rivieras.

Horizon Leisure Tours, c.1960s
This leaflet comes complete with 'picto-map' and brilliant hand-drawn graphics.

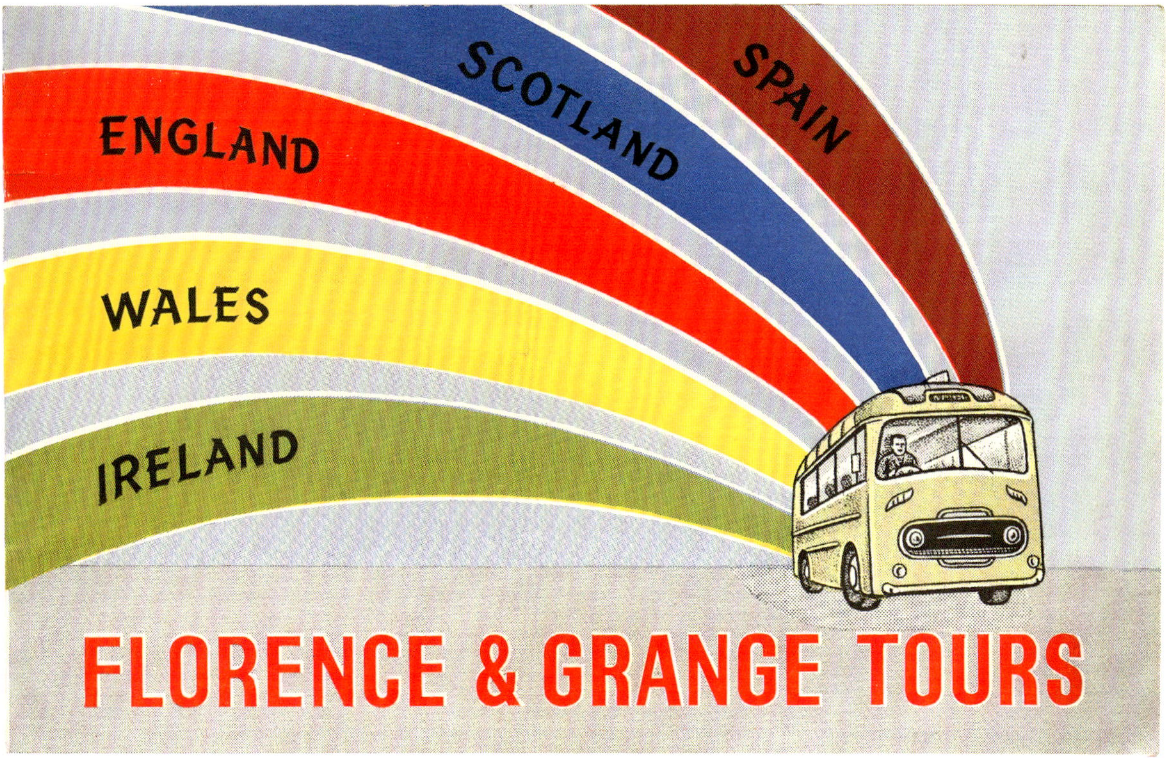
SCOTLAND
SPAIN
ENGLAND
WALES
IRELAND
FLORENCE & GRANGE TOURS

Horizon
air and coach
LEISURE TOURS
Horizon
cruises
featuring the new DAY-BY-DAY PICTO-MAP

GERMANY
£22-4-6
ITALY
£29-10-6
AUSTRIA
£28-19-6
SWITZERLAND
£29-19-6
SPAIN
£29-19-6
VISTA
LUXURY TOURS
1961
Continental
luxury
holidays by
VISTA

Vista Luxury Tours, 1961
I think the idea of luxury now compared to back then is radically different. Although some coaches still have those glass-panelled roof sections.

Vista Tours, 1965
'Vista Take You All The Way'. If you fancy the trip to Tossa de Mar then I guess that's a good thing. Nice use of two colour over-printing across her face.

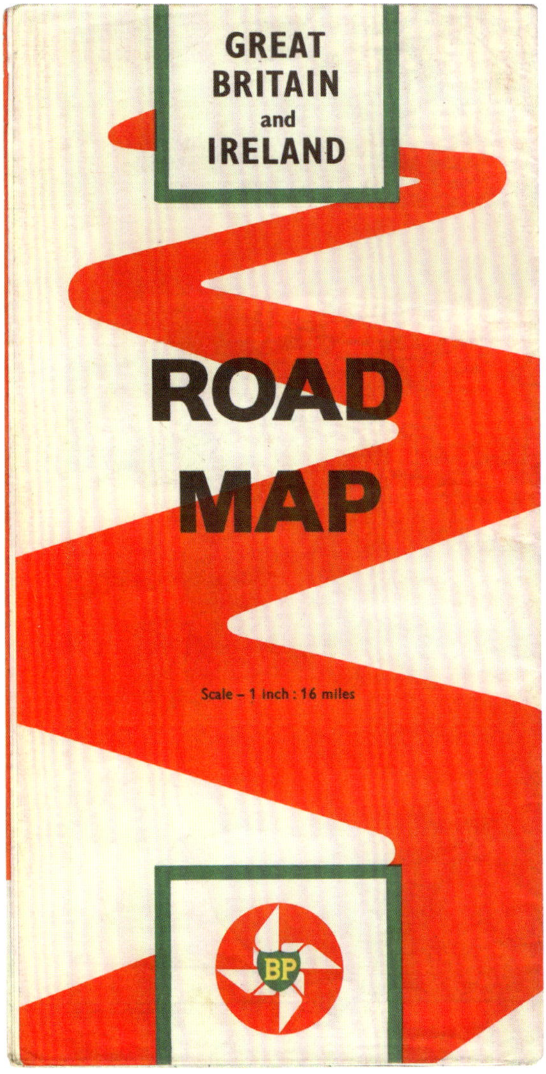

BP Road Maps, 1960s
These maps included ferry routes and highway code information, alongside the all-important 'Perpetual Lighting-Up Timetable' (the times when drivers were legally required to have their lights on). And all with odd graphic covers.

Bus Tours in Britain, 1960s
This impressively compact and competitive brochure brings together all the UK coach operators to fight it out in black and white.

Coach Wise in Britain, 1950s
'No matter when you are travelling, Winter or Summer, you need have no fear of maybe having to stand.' A great leaflet with hand-drawn illustrations, made in a style that has never really gone out of style.

a.m or p.m?, late 1960s
Without doubt this is the best brochure ever made to inform bus passengers that timetables will be moving to a 24-hour clock.

Continental Coach Tours, 1960s
Some very adventurous holidays offered here, including a 20-day camping tour around Europe: 2,200 miles, and every single one organised by the Bristol Omnibus Company. My kind of 1960s colour palette.

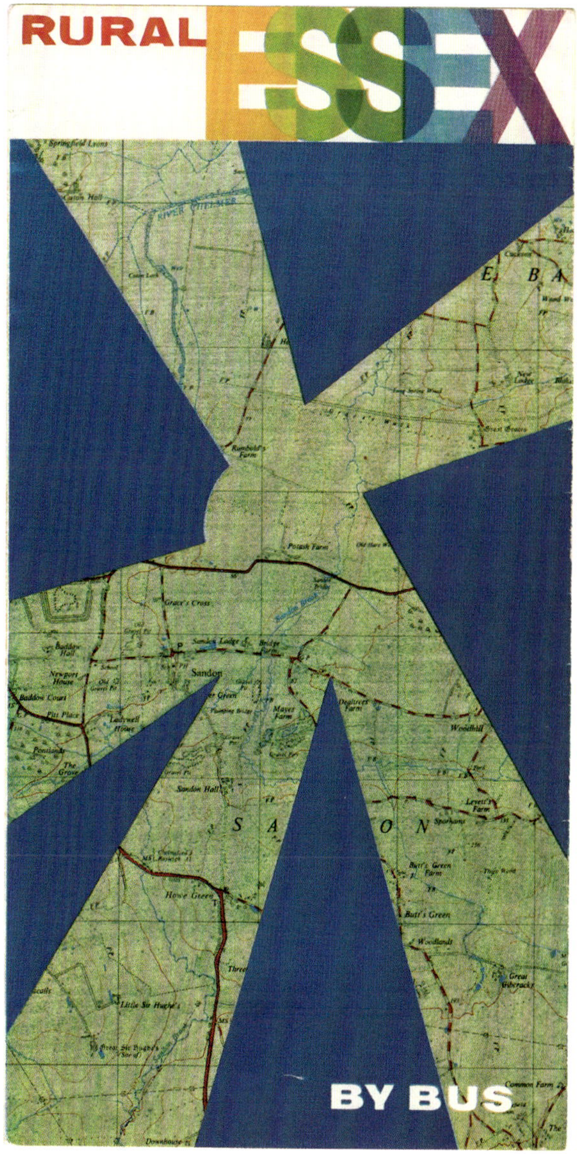

East Kent Maidstone and District, 1970s
How can they help? Well, there's an open-top service, a senior citizens fare-saver package and there's none of the fuss about parking.

Rural Essex By Bus, 1960s
Quite a radical design for a bus leaflet. Looks way better than anything you'll see out of the bus window.

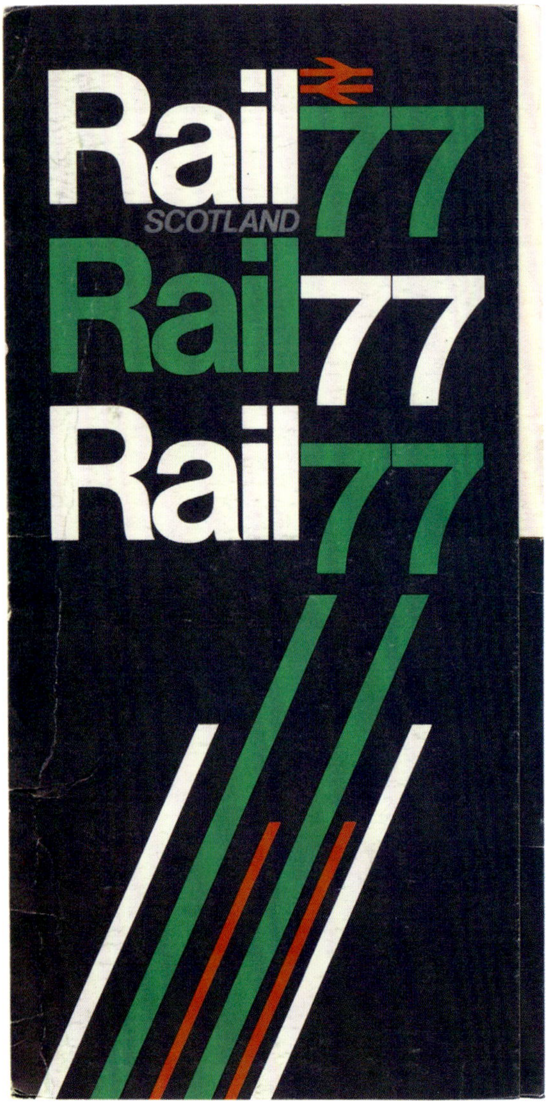
Rail77
SCOTLAND
Rail77
Rail77

Rail route. Inverness | Kyle of Lochalsh

Rail 77, 1977
A folder for all your Scotland 'Rail 77' tickets, timetables and brochures. 'Rail 77 is for people going places'. Well I never. Seems like British Rail got themselves some radical new graphics; these are likely by designer Bill Willison.

Inverness / Kyle of Lochalsh, 1977
A historic train journey through the heart of the Scottish Highlands really does require a well-written, well-researched and finely illustrated booklet. This is it.

Summer Railaway '75, '76, '77
Three leaflets for summer outings via Glasgow station via train, to such places as the Solway Firth, the Lake District, the Highland Games and best of all there's a 'Mystery Tour'.

Weekend Ticket, 1967
To a generation who got old without ever really being young, like the couple on the front of this brochure, British Rail were suggesting that 'Weekend travel can be fun'. Classic period two-colour graphics on display here.

Above: Golden Rail, 1972
Right: Bognor Regis, 1973
An interesting and quite successful campaign by British Rail, 'Golden Rail' was economic holiday rail travel (plus approved accommodation), but set in first-class carriages. With a whiff of Sainsbury's Own Label cereal packets here...

Golden Rail
Personal Choice Holidays 1973
Bognor Regis

Britrail Pass, 1976
The InterCity 125 high-speed train was reliable and fast, representing a paradigm shift in UK rail travel. It was the star of several British Rail brochure covers following its introduction in 1976.

Gatwick Railair Link, 1978
More groovy, period British Rail graphics by Bill Willison.

Business Travel by British Rail, 1960s
This brochure sells surprisingly affluent travel services on Pullman De-Luxe Diesel trains (known as the 'Blue Pullmans' due to their 'Nanking blue' livery). Classy food, a fine-looking buffet car, even posh, British, transport hotels. Ultimately, they were too expensive to maintain and were finally withdrawn from service in 1973.

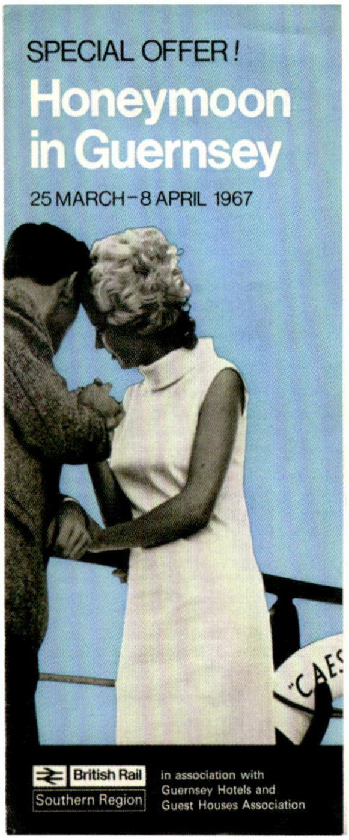
SPECIAL OFFER !
Honeymoon in Guernsey
25 MARCH – 8 APRIL 1967
British Rail
Southern Region
in association with Guernsey Hotels and Guest Houses Association

Fare Deals
TOGETHER TICKETS
Saturday Awayday Returns
3 January to 10 April 1976
from: Swansea · Neath · Port Talbot · Bridgend · Cardiff · Newport

GO MERRYMAKER
by train with
'Round Robin'
Super Circular
Rail Rides
May '79 – May '80
London Midland

European
Rail Traffic Office
PASSENGER
DIRECTORY
EUROPE

British Rail
Irish Seaways
Holiday highway to Ireland
Stranraer
Larne
The shortest sea route
Sailing and connecting rail services from 28 April to 30 September 1969.

INTER RAIL 81
Discover Europe and Morocco
by train and ship
Inter Rail freedom for the under 26's
One month's unlimited travel
in Europe for just £92*
available to 31 December 1981
*Subject to alteration due to currency fluctuations. Supplements are payable on some trains.

British Rail Leaflets, 1960s–1980s
A series of late British Rail offers and graphic information leaflets, including round-robin trips by train, your honeymoon in Guernsey and the number for Cyril Davis, the manager at Swansea Travel Centre.

Anglo Scottish Car Carrier, 1962
This daytime version of the 'car sleeper service', allowed you to load your car onto the covered wagon in London, then drive away in Newcastle or Edinburgh later the same day.

Rail Rover Tickets, 1962
These tickets offered seven days unlimited travel across Somerset, Devon and Cornwall for just £5. An 'All Line' ticket, giving passengers unlimited travel across the UK for a week, was only £17.

Another Side of Scotland, c.1967
This guided tour of Scotland leaflet was produced by a knitwear company. With subtle, illustrated hints, as to which knit to wear at each location.

Shetland, 1963, 1966 (right)
These fascinating period guides to the isles include pages of local adverts promoting everything from 'Ronnie's Red and White Taxis' to 'The Woolie Horse' on which to stretch or dry knitwear. Superb stained-glass-window-style artwork.

SHETLAND

Belfast, Official Tourist Handbook, 1966
A city that has it all – Guinness, stock car racing and a brand new Post Office Headquarters. Photograph-filled typography is one of my favourite graphic design styles.

Stirling, 1970
This informative brochure for the fine historic city, utilises an 18th-century map.

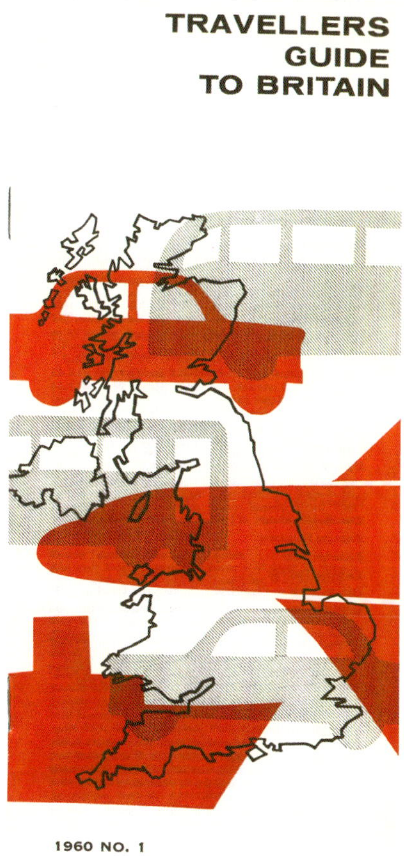

Britain Events, 1967
This cover features the incredible Up Helly Aa Festival, a celebration of Norse heritage, which takes place in Lerwick on the Shetland Isles. A torch-bearing procession culminates in the burning of a Viking galley ship.

Travellers Guide to Britain, 1960
Published for the USA and Canada, this leaflet includes a wealth of vital facts, but most importantly, licensing hours. A lovely two-colour, paired-back design.

London quick guide and map

London Quick Guide, 1970
This quick guide only has time to mention one London pub – Ye Olde Cheshire Cheese on Fleet Street. The bold front cover employs cunning use of collage, scale, and restrained colour.

Places of Interest in and around London, c.1964
When I first saw this booklet I immediately thought it could well be a subtle, graphic representation of London smog.

Which? Holiday, London, 1979
Useful monthly magazine for holidaymakers, with a great flat-colour scheme for the cover.

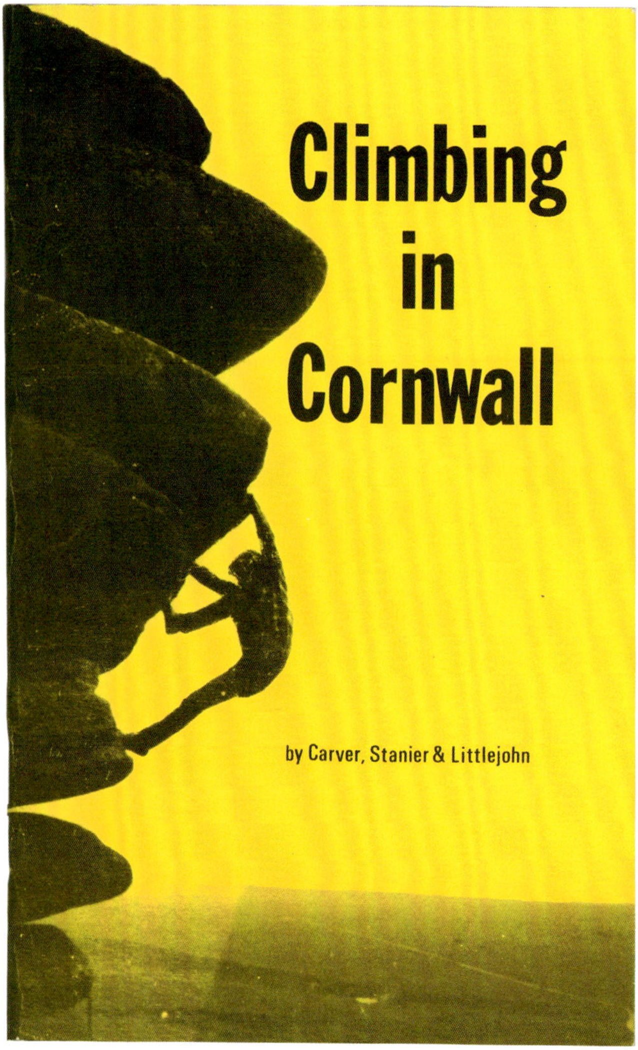

Climbing in Cornwall, 1973
A charming and confident guide to Cornish ascents. Includes routes, approaches, maps, climb grading, etc. This artwork could not be any simpler or more perfect: a great photograph, matched with restrained typography and design.

Dartmoor National Park, c.1967
Not the official guide book, merely a small pocket guide. Note that 'feeding the ponies is dangerous'.

Holiday in Britain, 1967
The graphic vibe of Swinging London manifests itself in a holiday brochure. This free guide was produced by the British Travel Association. 'Whatever your idea of holiday heaven, you can find it in Britain'.

HOLIDAY IN BRITAIN 1967

HOLIDAY IN BRITAIN 1967

Countryside Commission Trail Maps, 1976
A very fine set of maps, all using the acorn 'waymark sign' as the perfect graphic device. Sadly the waymark sign itself is not attributed to a specific designer.

Ordnance Survey Maps, 1970
This lovely set of OS maps, with their distinctive illustrations, were the first in the series to be changed to 1:50,000 scale.

Ordnance Survey
OS
Exmoor
Showing part of National Park Boundary
Tourist Map
£2·20
The area covered by the map is indicated on the back cover

Ordnance Survey
OS
New Forest
Showing New Forest Boundary
Tourist Map
58p
The area covered by the map is indicated on the back cover

Ordnance Survey
OS
Peak District
Showing National Park Boundary
Tourist Map
10/- [50p]

Ordnance Survey
OS
Lake District
Showing part of National Park Boundary
Tourist Map
55p
The area covered by the map is indicated on the back cover

English Holidays, 1975
Shot like a 'hazy mist' erotic photograph, in the style of David Hamilton (1933–2016), this brochure gave me the impression that everyone in the shires wears Laura Ashley and is constantly in the pub.

Holiday in Britain, 1961
Not sure I can think of a worse holiday back in 1961. However, this large brochure is full of thatched cottages, kids leapfrogging on beaches and busy winter gardens. Perhaps it wasn't that bad after all.

Holiday England, 1971
Taking inspiration from the late 1960s psychedelia, this cover has an exciting dash of Bonnie MacLean's Fillmore posters about it. Unfortunately, I'm disappointed to report that inside it's just plain old England. Even an interview with BBC television presenter Cliff Michelmore (1919–2016) cannot disguise that fact.

HF Summer Holidays, 1963
We can thank the father of the Open-Air Movement, Thomas Arthur Leonard (1864–1948), for establishing the Holiday Fellowship back in 1913. His simple belief was that holidays should be about celebrating the great outdoors. HF Holidays still thrives today.

Isle of Man, 1966
This small leaflet boasted that holidays in the Isle of Man were all about the over-crowded promenade and incredibly busy beaches. Neither of these points are really selling it to me.

Isle of Thanet, 1979
Get the bus to the wonderful Isle of Thanet (which is, strictly speaking, a peninsula and part of Kent). Bring your bikini, there are fairgrounds and a model village.

Isle of Man

The wonderful
Isle of
THANET
Edinburgh
Manchester
London
Thanet
Broadstairs · Margate · Ramsgate

Mid Wales, 1973
A map and information, the artist responsible for the fine cover artwork (and some interior vignettes) is sadly uncredited.

Wallace Arnold Holidays, 1964
The straightforward use of a vivid colour palette makes this brochure for UK-based coach tours possibly the most joyous I have ever read.

Margate, c.1960
A fine introduction to the Thanet area, with an unbelievably long list of hotels and boarding houses that are probably now hipster rentals or second homes.

There's something in the air
AT
MARGATE
TICKETS
AT
FRAMES,
WOLVERHAMPTON
BIRCHINGTON
WESTGATE-ON-SEA
WESTBROOK
MARGATE
CLIFTONVILLE

Butlinland Pwllheli postcard, 1968
Dear Mum, hope you are keeping well. We are still enjoying ourselves. Plenty to do. See you soon. Ken

Butlinland Minehead postcard (top), 1968
The weather here is lovely and everyone is having a great time. Lots to do so you can't get bored. Thanks for the money. Love Sal

Butlinland Minehead postcard, 1968
Dear Mum, arrived alright. Plenty to do. Weather nice. See you soon love Susan

Butlinland Bognor Regis postcard, 1968
Dear Carol, having a nice time, weather lovely, enjoying ourselves. Done most things in the camp. Will write later to see how you are getting on. From Jane

Pontin Rent-A-Chalet, 1969
These were brilliantly conceived holiday camps with everything you could wish for in-house, including a concrete playground (they were all like that back then).

Ribble Holiday Tours, 1970
Detailing comprehensive UK-wide coach and hotel tours, departing from 31 separate locations in the north of England. This year saw the introduction of a new fleet of coaches. The design of these two Ribble brochures was certainly heading in a fresher graphic direction than other holiday coach tour companies of the time.

Ribble Centred Holidays, 1970
Further adventures on coach-based holidays to popular destinations in the UK and Europe. My favourite itinerary is for the London holiday: 'First Day – travel to London by Express coach. Other Days – Free in London. Last Day – return travel from London by Express Coach.'

Ribble Centred Holidays, 1969
'Centred' means a holiday for people who like to stay in one resort. I'd like to visit the swimming pool on the front, but annoyingly, there are no clues inside as to its location.

Southport, 1972
Brilliant, folk-like, hand-drawn guide to the exciting sport events and social gatherings taking place in Southport.

Ribble
CENTRED HOLIDAYS
1969

holiday in
YORKSHIRE
PRICE: ONE SHILLING AND SIXPENCE

Holidays in Yorkshire, 1968
One shilling and sixpence bought you the keys to the UK's largest county and a list of all hotels and campsites for the perfect break. Including information on pony trekking.

Holiday Haunts, 1974
The Great Western Railway's comprehensive annual guide to holiday destinations across England and Wales. Established in 1906, it included guest houses, restaurant guides, maps and more.

Newquay, 1966
This large guide to Newquay and its immediate surroundings makes you realise that, even back then, the area was way ahead in the surfing game. Front and back of brochure shown here.

Sunspot
SUMMER HOLIDAYS BY SCHEDULED AIR SERVICES
FROM MANCHESTER, LIVERPOOL, LEEDS, NEWCASTLE AND LONDON
ARRANGED BY HOLIDAY & COMMERCIAL TRAVEL LTD.
1st April 1968 to 31st October 1968

Sunspot, 1968
This brochure, with a slightly apocalyptic, disaster-movie feel, was produced by Manchester-based holiday operator Sunspot. Where the Costa Blanca and Costa Brava, costa not mucha.

Mutual Tours, c.1964
A short-lived publication for international travel to the sun by coach. The cover illustration could be a flyer for a 1980s acid-house party.

Sea Sun Fun Holidays, 1965
Ten days in the Venetian or Spanish Riviera from £22. This price includes the very special 'candlelight social'.

The THF Holiday Planner, c.1970
This leaflet is a slight anti-climax, as it turns out it's just a quick booking form for Trusthouse Forte hotels in and around the UK. Like the old Victorian pile they had in Russell Square.

Air Plan Holidays, 1960
A progressive new travel company from Cambridge, offering chartered coaches and planes to European rivieras. Odd but pleasing totemic design.

AIR
PLAN
HOLIDAYS
HILLS TOURS LTD.
BOOKING AGENCY:
OLD MEETING ST.
WEST BROMWICH.
1960

B·O·A·C
SUNSHINE
HOLIDAYS
WORLD
WIDE
SUMMER 1965

HOLY LAND TOURS
To ATHENS
LEBANON
THE HOLY LAND
ROME
BY AIR
WITH
B·O·A·C
AND
HOLY LAND TOURS LIMITED
17 Coventry Street, Piccadilly, London, W.1
GERrard 7524

INGHAMS
1966/7 WINTER SUN
HOLIDAYS

BOAC Sunshine Holidays World Wide, 1965
Modern holiday companies would do well to adopt the cool, fun, laid-back graphic approach found in this brochure.

Holy Land Tours, early 1960s
'The Greatest Story Ever Told', but in a holiday format.

Inghams WinterSun, 1966
Established by adventurous traveller Walter Ingham in 1934, this company, which is still going strong today, specialises in winter sun and skiing holidays.

Fourways of London, 1960
This novelty die-cut brochure was obviously successful, as they used the same design for the next two years.

Co-Operative Travel Service, 1962, 1963
The history of this service can be traced back to the Co-Op Excursions Department. Established in 1905, its mission was to find members the best travel deals. Some fun, felt-tip, cover illustrations.

HOLIDAYS
1963
IN
GREAT
BRITAIN
AND
ABROAD
PRESENTED BY
CO-OPERATIVE
TRAVEL
SERVICE
C.W.S.
C.W.S.

R.A.S. Holidays, 1974
This Rambler's Association Services brochure for 1974 has a surprisingly large range. I thought they just walked around the UK, but no, they ramble across the entire globe.

JET Holidays, c.1960s
Coach and air joy throughout Europe, beginning in Birmingham.

Summer Serenade, 1958
In the late 1950s, this pioneering company were already offering the most extraordinary trips across the whole of Europe, including sports-focussed breaks.

Progressive Tours – Holidays Abroad, 1966
Using simple, modern graphics, this innovative holiday company, offered trips to the German Democratic Republic, Mongolia and Poland, all easily bookable with a £5 deposit.

Progressive
TOURS
HOLIDAYS ABROAD · 1966

Eurail Guide, 1974
A dense and comprehensive timetable of all rail travel across Europe. The best thing about this is the unfinished Caran d'Ache-style colour pen illustration, which could easily be the winning entry of a 'draw our new cover' competition.

Paris and the French Ports by Train and Ship, 1969
Travelling from Folkestone, Dover and Newhaven to the continent, via something called a 'boat train'.

Overland Super-Rail, 1970
Offering 8- and 15-day 'escorted' trips by train to Belgium, Spain, Italy or Austria. I'm very much enjoying the unexpected, white-train graphic, steaming directly towards us.

Overleaf: Frontier 1972
Lively budget group holidays for 'people going places', including a nine-week European tour.

Townsend Thoresen, 1972
Car ferry booklet with routes and timing from Southampton and Dover. A smorgasbord is served on a number of the Southampton crossings. Nice use of Matchbox toys.

Overland
Super-Rail
Holidays by train
Summer 1970
Belgium 17gns
Spain 30gns
Italy 35gns
Austria 34gns
8

1972
FRONTIER

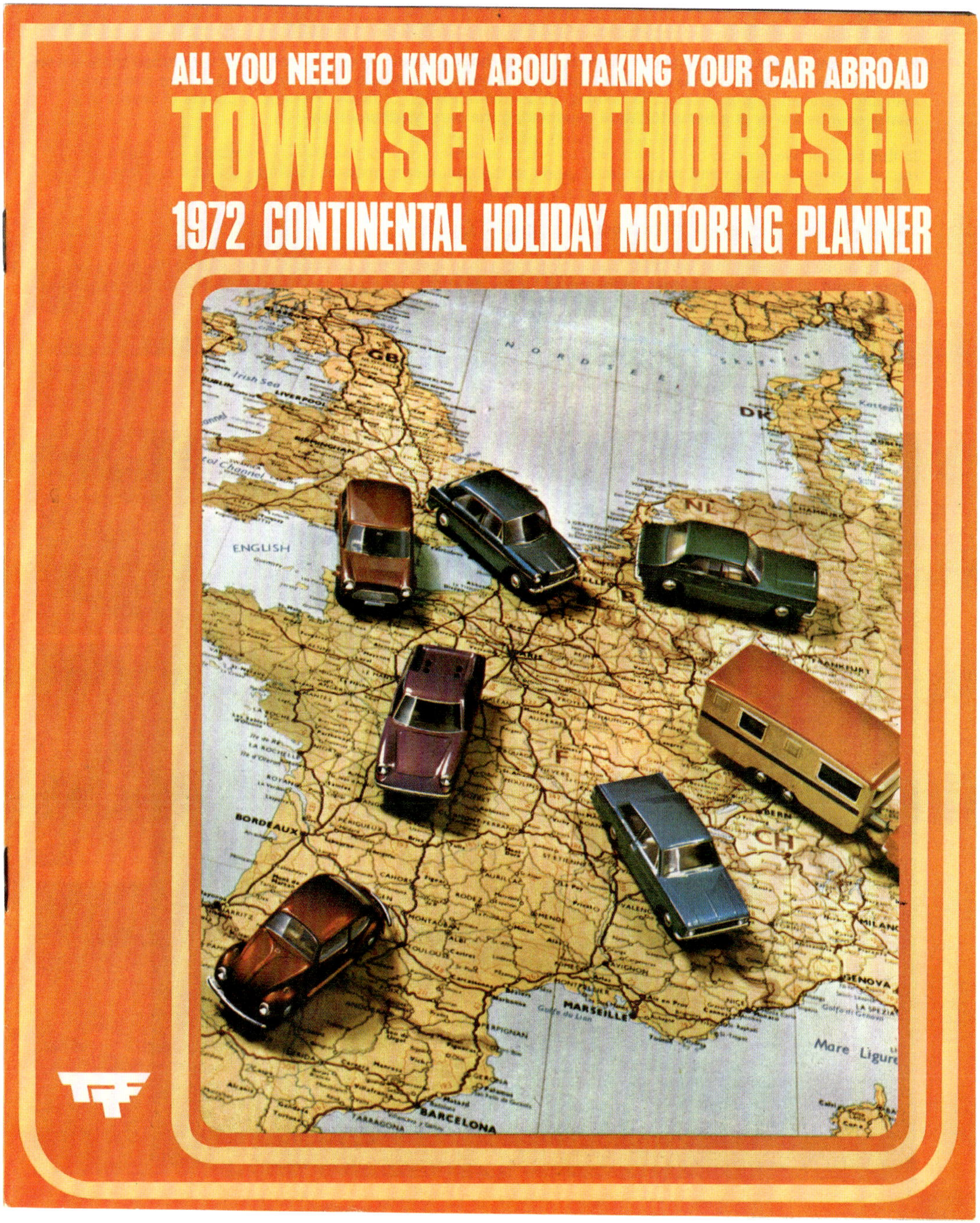
ALL YOU NEED TO KNOW ABOUT TAKING YOUR CAR ABROAD
TOWNSEND THORESEN
1972 CONTINENTAL HOLIDAY MOTORING PLANNER

Youth Hostels Handbook 1966, 1967
This invaluable guide to all the YHA establishments contains invaluable information, including where and how to receive postal mail as you travel around the hostel network.

The Youth Hosteller, 1967, 1968
Originally called *The Rucksack*, the monthly YHA magazine for the active youth hostel user includes trip ideas, updates on accommodation, brass-rubbing events and, by the looks of it, some potholing action (no thanks). The publication still exists, but now known as *The Journey*. Good, clean, simple design meets great period colours.

Come Hostelling, 1971
It seems so obvious now, but youth hostels were where all the fashionable young men used to hang out back then.

Hostelling Abroad, 1981
YHA members could travel to any country in the world with a youth hostel organisation and get a bed for just £1.75 a night.

Highway Map of Alaska, 1975
This map and guide suggests some odd adventures, such as 'friendly confrontations' with seals.

Alaska USA, 1977
This leaflet includes details of the annual 'Fur Rendezvous'.

Alaska! Traveller's List, 1972
An exhaustive and deftly illustrated record of all airlines, buses and taxis in Alaska.

What's Up in Alaska, 1974
A year-round list of unmissable cultural events, including 'Dog Week' (September), the Cat Club Annual Show (February) and the Salmon Derby (May).

Meteor Crater, 1967
Apparently discovered by 'white men' in 1871. Right. A deft combination of photographs and amateur illustration brings the impressive landmark to life.

Amazing Arizona, 1973
A fascinating map and guide, which cunningly divides Arizona into different regions based on climate, terrain and recreational opportunities.

The Great Meteor Crater, c.1960
An earlier leaflet promoting the same crater, allegedly, the 'world's first proven'. With a depth of 570 feet and a 3-mile circumference.

Colorado Rockies, c.1960
This classic tour includes Wheaties for breakfast and a visit to Buffalo Bill's grave.

Grand Canyon National Park, 1961
Totally awe inspiring, even in black and white.

Bear Country USA, 1968
Sage advice from this wildlife park in the Black Hills of South Dakota: 'Stay in your cage with the windows up'.

Greyhound Bus, c.1960s
These Greyhound bus guides cover no less than 100,000 miles of scenic American highways. This American institution, founded in 1914, reached a highpoint from the 1930s to the 1950s, when the company built Streamline Moderne-style terminals for their fleets of classic Silverside busses (with aluminium sides). Today the company still operates, covering over 2,400 destinations.

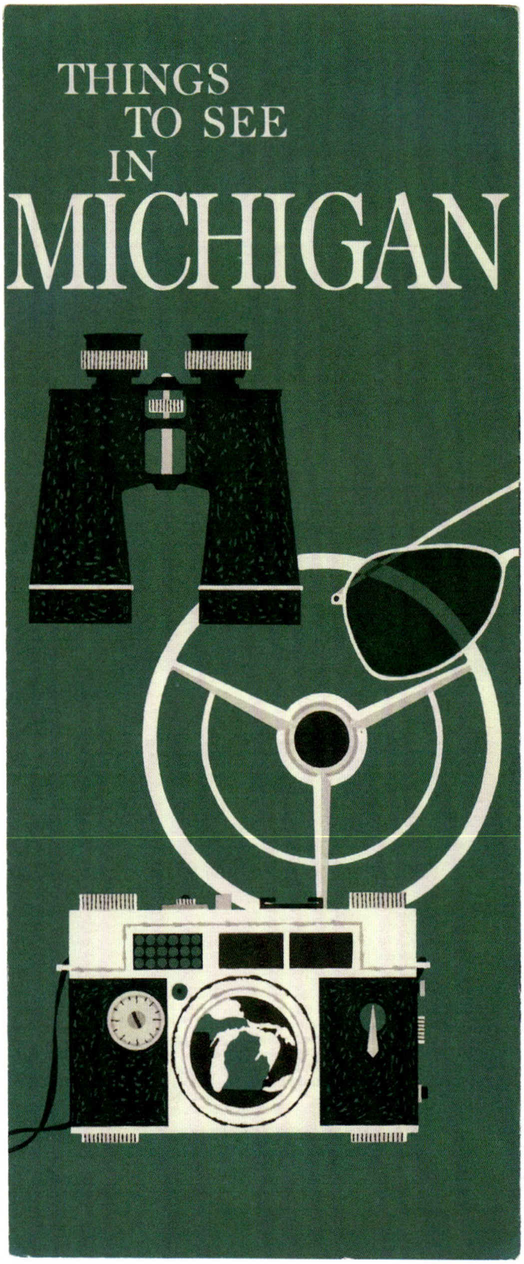

Things to See in Michigan, 1966
The map inside this leaflet looked like a dot to dot puzzle, but no, it marks 53 places of note to visit. Including a music camp and the Gerber Baby Food factory.

Hoover Dam, 1972
Information about 'one of the seven wonders of the world'. The dam structure contains 3 ¼ million tons of concrete.

Zion National Park, Utah, 1962
A mere 147,000 acres of trails and spectacular canyons.

Utah Motel Guide, 1962
'Our fine highways will lead you to thriving modern cities and ghost towns.'

USA, Houlders World Holidays, 1969
Introducing the all-new Pan Am Air Clipper service, or Boeing 747 ('Jumbo Jet'), a plane so big it reduced ticket prices by a third.

I know it's an obvious devise, but I'm sure the couple in the centre will be visiting all those little segments surrounding them.

Travel a New World, 1967
This ambitious leaflet has a fold-out mileage table that is the size of a small town.

Nevada Utah, 1979
An American Automobile Association map that includes directions to the US military nuclear testing site.

Tour Louisiana, c.1960s
A warm welcome is guaranteed in this year-round vacationland.

Aquarena Springs, 1969
A waterful wonderland? In Texas? Includes information on a Submarine Theatre and Grist Mill, and quite possibly some psychedelics based on the artwork.

Silver Springs, c.1960
Nature's underwater fairyland, with jungle cruises, glass-bottom boat trips and rattlesnake milking.

How to Find the Action, 1972
A lovely glossy white brochure with a brown buff textured interior. The 'action' referred to here includes shopping malls, skin diving and a waxworks museum.

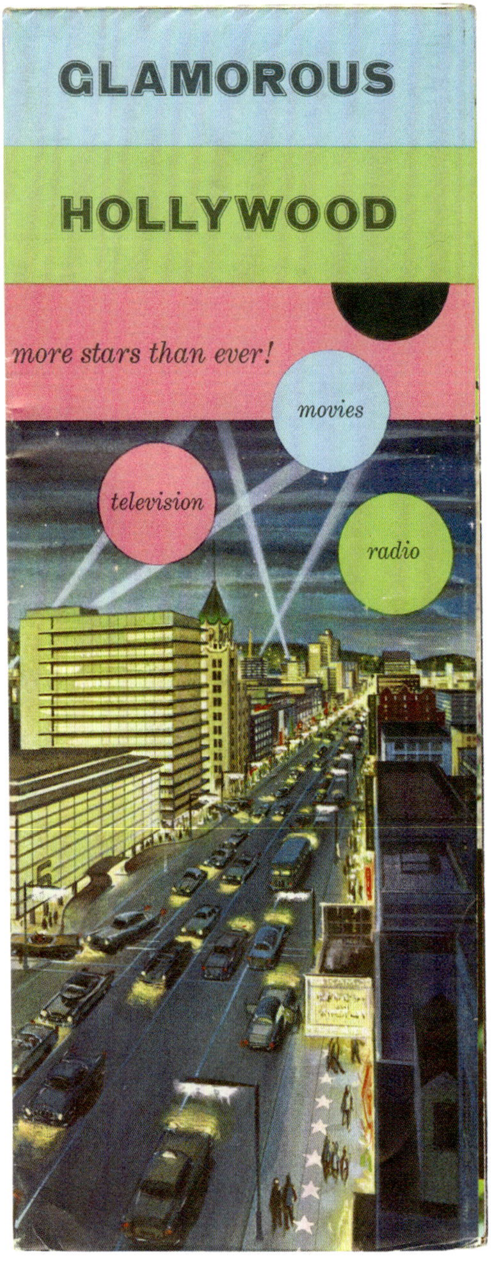

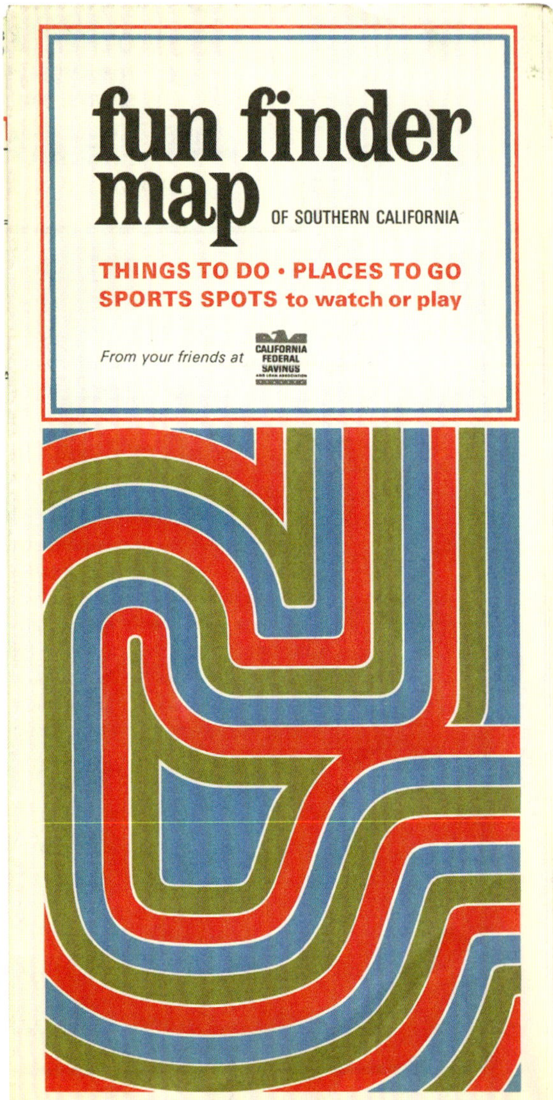

Glamorous Hollywood, c.1950s
A remarkably plain fold-out map and informational leaflet, not quite befitting the 'glamour capitol of the world'.

Fun Finder Map, 1968
An oddly abstracted map with golf courses, sports fields and racetracks, all floating around the Los Angeles area. Superb cover graphic, winning for both its vibrant colours and wacked-out design.

... More Fun for Everyone in Seattle, 1965
According to this colourful promotion, as well as the incredible Space Needle, Seattle offers sport, theatre, golf, horse racing and pirates.

Las Vegas Gray Line, 1979
If you ask me, it's probably better to see Vegas from the coach window without bothering to get off.

New York in The Fall, 1974
A small, quarterly, comprehensive guide to New York City's rich arts and cultural scene.

Manhattan Bus Guide, 1974
The New York City Transit Authority graphic standards, designed by Massimo Vignelli and Bob Noorda of Unimark International in 1970, remains a classic. This leaflet includes various loop rides where you can hop on and off as many times as you wish for just $1.

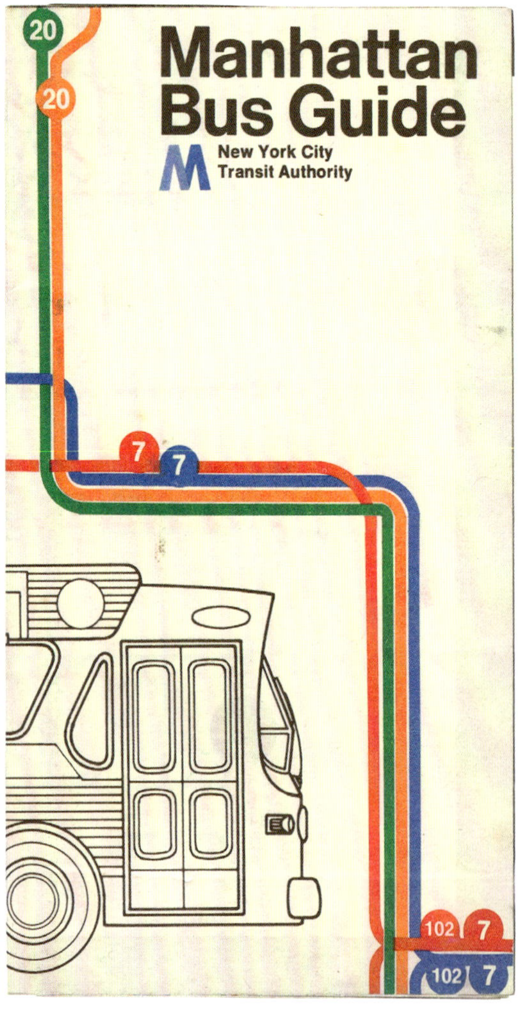

New York Begins at the World Trade Center, 1986
'For high drama, nothing tops the World Trade Center'. A free pamphlet from the Port Authority.

Welcome to the World Trade Center, 1977
A great early small-format brochure containing a panoramic viewing-platform fold-out map.

Hotel Plitvice, 1963
You may not have spotted the 'P' in this artful design. I hadn't and so I'd been looking for the Hotel Litvice for quite a while.

Hotel Lev, c.1965
A fold-out brochure from a classy hotel in the Slovenian capital, featuring metallic gold printing with a hint of modernism.

Dalmatia Yugoslavia, c.1965
'Stay with a friend', it says. Is that my friend on the front?

Yugoslavia, c.1965
Fine cultural pamphlet. The front cover photograph might well have been taken at the Light Metal Factory in Ražice.

Yougoslavie: L'Adriatique Ensoleille, 1968
A lovely French sales brochure (Yugoslavia: The Sunny Adriatic), I'm very much drawn to the pagan sun god depicted here.